THE TRUTH ABOUT DIGITAL MARKETING FOR FINANCIAL ADVISORS

How to Create a Magnetic, Authentic Brand that Unlocks Unparalleled Growth for your Firm

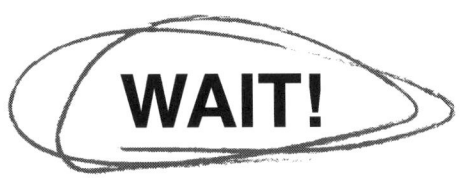

Don't start reading without...

1. Taking a few seconds to visit: www.truthaboutdm.com/starthere
2. Downloading the *Top 106 Truths About Digital Marketing* cheatsheet
3. Watching this personal video introduction and book summary

The truth is...
No one has the time for another business book full of fluff.

The value starts now.

The Truth About Digital Marketing for Financial Advisors © Copyright <<2022>> Kristin Shea-Jebeile

All rights reserved. No part of this publication may be reproduced, distributed, or transmitted in any form or by any means, including photocopying, recording, or other electronic or mechanical methods, without the prior written permission of the publisher, except in the case of brief quotations embodied in critical reviews and certain other noncommercial uses permitted by copyright law.

Although the author and publisher have made every effort to ensure that the information in this book was correct at press time, the author and publisher do not assume and hereby disclaim any liability to any party for any loss, damage, or disruption caused by errors or omissions, whether such errors or omissions result from negligence, accident, or any other cause.

Adherence to all applicable laws and regulations, including federal, state and local governing professional licensing, business practices, advertising, and all other aspects of doing business in the US, Canada or any other jurisdiction is the sole responsibility of the reader.

ISBN: 979-8-9862951-3-8

Are you a top-performing independent advisor & CEO who has become a victim of their own success?

✴ *Symptoms include:*

- Feeling like your business owns you, instead of the other way around
- A lack of freedom and time to focus on the high-value activities that drives your firm forward
- Being the bottleneck inside your business as you balance running the firm, planning for the future, being the primary decision-maker, while also meeting with clients and managing the day to day

✴ *You are also likely to agree with one (or all) of the following:*

- "I'm afraid I've been trading years of my life for production trophies."
- "I know that cookie-cutter solutions and shiny marketing objects will not solve my problems."
- "I'm tired of being the smartest person in the room."
- "I want a partnership that treats me like 1 of 1, instead of 1 of 10,000."
- "I'm afraid to grow any bigger."

If so, it might make sense to have a conversation with my team at Triad Partners.

www.truthaboutdm.com/apply

At Triad Partners, we help elite advisors achieve scale *(a.k.a. unlimited growth & freedom* in their business and life).

In fact, we've proven that top advisors can achieve scale faster and easier than they ever thought possible.

IF YOU ARE:

✓ Hungry for the next big breakthrough in your business and life

✓ Focused on surrounding yourself with other leaders who challenge, inspire, and help you to do and be best you can be

✓ A comprehensive planner doing more than $10 million a year in FIA's

(...and you're not getting a ton of value, innovation, or high-level business development support from your FMO...)

Let's have a conversation.

www.truthaboutdm.com/apply

MEET KRISTIN

Kristin Shea, RICP®, is an award-winning and highly sought-after consultant, speaker, and influencer on a mission to serve and change the independent financial advisor space.

Kristin accidentally found herself in financial services after dropping out of college and accepting a job offer by two regulars at the restaurant where she waited tables.

As a student of psychology/economics and a natural born artist and connector, Kristin fell in love with the industry and opportunity to change lives in our communities and help advisors do one major thing:

Build a practice that blesses your life instead of becoming it.

In an industry that is saturated with ineffective solutions and marketing advice, Kristin has dedicated her career to delivering the art of digital marketing and CEO coaching to forward-thinking financial advisors.

Known for her honest voice and sense of humor, Kristin delivers a clear roadmap to scaling your practice, standing out from the herd, and creating success online.

DEDICATION ♡

For Every Advisor Who...

Knows they need to be online but doesn't know where to start.

Is sick of being "sold" digital solutions that don't work and is craving the results they know are possible.

Wants a business with unlimited growth potential—but also creates more freedom in their lives.

Has put it all on the line because you know that the ability to create better financial outcomes means making the world a better place for years to come.

For the People.

Because better messaging and marketing by advisors is key to helping more people find financial peace and fulfillment—which I believe results in happier, healthier, and more empowered communities.

For Anyone and Everyone Else...

With a dream of doing something you never thought was possible, and on a mission to make the world a better place and spread love and light.

For my beautiful brother Michael.

You can do anything you set your mind, or massive heart, to.

ACKNOWLEDGMENTS

I want to start off by thanking my advisor community.

There are just too many to name, but if you think (for even a second) that this might include you, it probably does. To every advisor I've worked with, currently work with, or crossed paths with. If this book helps you, inspires you, serves you even just a fraction of how much you all have inspired and served me, I've done my job.

Everything I have, and everything I do, comes from your continued trust, good energy, and support. You do one of the most important jobs on the entire planet and your clients are so lucky to have you. I love and cherish you all more than you know.

My husband, Joe Jebeile.

Thank you for the sacrifices you've made so I can follow my dreams. Thank you for being there to celebrate every win and give me grace when I'm in the thick of it. Thank you for always keeping me on my toes, having my back, and being my favorite person to do everything and nothing with. You are my rock, my soulmate, and my best friend. *It's you and me against the world.*

Mom, Dad, Lisa, & Tim.

My parents and bonus parents. Thank you for not giving up on me when I was a wild child and for dealing with the whiplash of me finding my way one shiny object at a time. For letting me make mistakes, trusting me, and loving me unconditionally. For teaching me what it means to love and be loved. To have a work ethic. Be a person of integrity. Embrace adventure, use the name tags of the people in the grocery store checkout lines, and always, ALWAYS get back up. For being my role models and always keeping God front and center.

Mr. Tom Kestler.

Tom, thank you for plucking me out of the restaurant and always believing in me. Thank you for being my mentor, my confidant, my work-dad, my friend. I have never met a wiser or more compassionate human (and leader!) and I am grateful to have sharpened my iron under your influence. On the days when I feel like an imposter, I always come back to the foundation you created for me as a professional and the confidence you inspired.

Shawn Sparks and Brad Johnson.

For inspiring me, challenging me, and empowering me. If someone would've told me early in my career that I would one day leave Virginia, move to Kansas, and become partners with either of you (let alone both of you!), I just wouldn't have believed it.

Thank you for your heart, vision, and inspiration. I don't know if I would've written this book without your support and encouragement. There is no one else I'd rather change the industry with.

Acknowledgments

My family at Triad Partners.

Just, *wow*. Creating something from scratch, changing an industry, and doing what no one else has ever done before is wild. Not every day has been easy, which makes being on this mission together that much more fulfilling. Regardless of where we go and what the future holds, our journey together is one of the most fulfilling things I've ever been a part of. Thank you for everything you do every single day. We are doing the damn thing!

Kim Harrington.

An early mentor and one of the most authentic people I've ever met. Thank you for encouraging and empowering me, even as a naive 21-year-old, to go against the status quo and think bigger about my role and the industry. Every single door that has been opened for me as a professional can be tied back to LinkedIn, and you were my first and biggest advocate for laying off the cold calls and leaning into digital.

My best friends.

Kaitlynn, Kerime, Becca, Sara, Sara, and Erin. My family by choice. The most meaningful work is that invested in the relationships that mean the most to you. Your friendship means the absolute world to me. Thank you for enriching my life in more ways than I'll ever have words for. Thanks for being such inspiring women. Thanks for doing life with me. Life would really suck without you guys.

Truth Is…There are just too many to name.

Miscellaneous contributors who have been invaluable to bringing this book to life and the mission at large: Michael Kitces, Michael Hyatt, Chris Smith, Kerk Murray, Chandler Bolt, John Ruhlin, Daniel Crosby, Ivy Hughes, Pat Szot, Rhett Joy, Adam Cmelja, Derek Notman, Reno Frazzitta, Joseph Cammayo, Jen Miklowski.

*Obligatory**
COMPLIANCE DISCLOSURE

As someone who does not work with clients, I have the sweet, sweet freedom of not *really* having to worry about compliance.

As a marketer at heart, it physically pains me to see lengthy disclosures on incredible—and compliant!—content.

With that said, I know I have a responsibility to not let *my* freedoms translate into reckless advice or a barrage of ideas that might get *you* in trouble. And I take that responsibility very seriously.

So, I do have some disclosures for content included in *The Truth About Digital Marketing for Financial Advisors.*

I'll be honest, getting my message dissected by compliance is not something I'm used to.

"What if the disclosures negatively affect readers' experience of the book?"

"How many of these are REALLY necessary?"

"Can I, like, hide these somewhere?

Any of that relatable? Or was that just me being a newbie?

And then, I remembered that this is something many of you battle daily.

I can deal with it. And getting in the trenches to fight the good fight alongside advisors is my jam.

So…Even though it's not *ideal*, I'm excited about the opportunity to make a big show about my disclosures before we get to the good stuff.

For everyone who has ever felt like a compliance requirement has detracted from your efforts and activities to add value—this one's for you:

1. For Financial Professional Use Only. This is not to be used with the general public.
2. Some of the names—specifically names of Triad Partners clients—have been changed to protect their identity and the sanctity of our exclusive community.
3. Any advisor I reference by their real name gave me prior authorization and was not compensated, bribed, harassed, or blackmailed into allowing me to share their stories.
4. Please, just follow the dang rules of your compliance department.

We good?

Moving on.

TABLE OF CONTENTS

Introduction 23

PART ONE:
Deconstructing the Past and Present of Digital Marketing for Advisors to Create the Foundation for Your Ideal Future

Chapter 1
The Professional Hills I'm Willing to Die On 33

Chapter 2
Funnels and Hurdles 59

Chapter 3
Vision 89

Chapter 4
Your Magnetic, Authentic Brand 115

Chapter 5
Alignment & Execution 147

PART TWO:

Creating Success Online & Unlocking Unlimited Growth Potential Using The Magnetic Digital Advisor Model™

Chapter 6
Materializing Your Online Relationships 177

Chapter 7
The Art of Addressing Your Audience 199

Chapter 8
Gains for Your Audience, Gains for You 217

Chapter 9
How to Nurture Your List 241

Chapter 10
Elevating Your Impact with Videos 261

Chapter 11
(Tailored) Content is King 279

Chapter 12
Social Media is an Investment 305

Chapter 13
Connecting the Dots 327

Conclusion and Next Steps 349

Introduction

When I first (and accidentally) got into the financial services industry in 2014, I was promoted from a college student waiting tables at Travinia Italian Kitchen and Wine Bar in Leesburg, Virginia to an annuity wholesaler at one of the industry's elite insurance marketing organizations (IMOs). The transition was sobering, to say the least.

I had a bit of an identity crisis. So much so that I literally dyed my hair black (I'm blonde)—not my best look.

Before dropping out of college to join the industry, I bounced between the majors that came easily to me: Psychology and communications. I always considered myself an artist and a free spirit. A proud millennial. A student of the people. A philanthropist and humanitarian. A bit of a rebel.

My new world was one of the last places I had envisioned myself ending up. Financial services? Really? Initially, I was disappointed in myself for conforming to The Man. Becoming a part of the machine. And my disdain grew as I came to understand how truly old school much of the financial services industry is, my new career included.

So, in my early days, when I was told that to be successful as an annuity wholesaler, which is a role that I have transitioned from as I am now a business coach—I had to essentially make 200,000 cold calls a day…I decided there had to be another—and dare I say, better—way.

It started off as an experiment.

Every Wednesday, I put my phone and dial list aside and instead spent the day playing around on LinkedIn.

My former boss and mentor, Kim, was encouraging. "What do you have to lose?"

I didn't have much of a game plan.

Although, if you know me on a personal level, you already know my first instinct is to shoot first, then aim.

Early on, I developed the following strategy: Sending messages to my ideal client asking for a 15-minute conversation to see if there was an opportunity for us to be more than a shallow LinkedIn connection. Calling it a strategy gives it too much credit, but it worked.

Fast forward almost a decade…I simply cannot imagine running my business without LinkedIn (or the other digital business development and social media tools that LinkedIn led me to).

Here's the thing: I know there are new hires in this industry, advisors included, being told that cold calling is still The Best Way to Grow Your Business. Cold calls aside, I'm sure you can relate to being led down a path, and sometimes pressured, to run your business the same way it would've been run 30 years ago despite your gut feeling that there may be a better way.

And, if we're being honest with ourselves, old habits die hard.

I now know from experience—not just from a hunch as a rebellious millennial, but by actual results—that there IS a better way.

Netflix proved it to Blockbuster.

YouTube proved it to cable.

Twitter proved it to the newspaper industry.

My mission is to help advisors just like you leverage digital marketing that automates how you fill your team's calendar, duplicates your ideal clients, and ultimately creates more freedom in your life.

> I want to help you unlock the potential of digital marketing in your firm so you can become *the ultimate rainmaker.*

But first, you have to believe that digital is the future, and the future is now.

Think about it.

Advisors have been coached for decades on the best way to grow their business. Cold calls and direct mail have been the reigning champions.

While these tactics are not *dead*, they certainly aren't the *future*.

The future is leveraging digital strategies to create an omnipresence for your firm that builds relationships with prospects by meeting your audience everywhere they are.

It means using tools that allow you to *instantaneously* connect with more people you could physically see in an entire month—or even an entire year.

The Internet, social media, and technology can do this, my friends.

Thanks to LinkedIn, many years of being a student, and almost a decade of grinding, I'm humbled to be recognized as one of the most prominent voices in the independent advisor space on all things related to marketing and growing and scaling your business. In fact, I'm now lovingly known as "That Girl on LinkedIn", or "LinkedIn Girl," for short.

Thanks to the true power of social media and technology, I've been able to leverage a platform that puts those possibilities on steroids.

I am not a digital marketer by trade. I am a business coach to the top 1% of independent advisors and fiduciaries in the country.

Yes, marketing is one way I add value to the offices I work with. But this is about so much more than digital marketing tactics.

It's about:

- ✓ Creating more fulfillment and joy in your business
- ✓ Increasing your revenue and your impact
- ✓ Creating the potential for unlimited growth in your firm and unlimited freedom in your life

And beyond that—I firmly believe that one of the shortcomings in our communities are related to financial literacy and the general public's apprehension to work with and trust financial advisors.

I believe that if our industry becomes better at marketing—a.k.a. connecting with and attracting our ideal audience—financial advisors have a better chance at creating a better world and stronger communities through better financial outcomes.

I aim to pull advisors out of the digital marketing dark so that they can rescue the people they serve from their own financial caves and into the light via financial literacy, empowerment, and enablement.

In *The Truth About Digital Marketing for Financial Advisors*, I will unveil how to use The CAVE Conversion Formula™ and The MAGNETIC Digital Advisor Model™ to help you build relationships and create authority within your ideal audience in your sleep by:

- ✓ Showing you how to build rinse-wash-repeat digital marketing systems that turns online strangers into raving fans
- ✓ Helping evaluate the digital marketing services you use and understand what does and doesn't work
- ✓ Teaching you how and why being yourself is the best way to attract your audience

- ✓ Showing you how to save time and open doors for exponential growth for your firm by creating more efficient processes, leveraging proven, scalable tactics used by of some of the best advisors, CEOs, and thought-leaders from both inside and outside our industry
- ✓ Illuminating what it takes to turn online conversations into real life appointments and revenue by understanding what is *actually* holding people back from pulling the trigger
- ✓ Helping you reframe the way you look at brand equity and increasing your business valuation if/when it's time to sell
- ✓ Explaining how to create outstanding, engaging content across multiple platforms
- ✓ *Giving you actionable next steps so you can get started today!*

If I do my job, and you do yours, *The Truth About Digital Marketing for Financial Advisors* will help you and your team (if you have one)—whether you're bringing on $5 tor $500 million dollars a year in new assets—not only be a better digital marketer but have a more efficient, valuable business without adding onto the weight of your firm that already rests on your shoulders.

Fair Warning (and Full Disclosure):

One of my team's core philosophies is: Check your ego at the door.

I won't pretend to have all the answers.

But! I am blessed to work with an elite and exclusive community of the highest performing offices in the independent space through my work at Triad Partners, an exclusive IMO known for business development and coaching. These firms have figured out scale, they're marketing masterminds, and bring on hundreds of millions of dollars annually. I learn something new from them every single day, and although I cannot list their names in the credits to protect their information/identities, they are my co-authors.

I also work with a group of world class experts—international best-sellers, renowned thought leaders, and the digital marketers who literally fill stadiums for household names—that Triad has partnered with to create cutting-edge business development for our advisors.

In *The Truth About Digital Marketing for Financial Advisors,* I'll provide resources, examples, and tools to add into your digital marketing toolbox based on my own experience and lessons gleaned from the top 1 percent of financial advisors in the U.S. and digital marketers on the planet. You will get:

- ✓ Behind the scenes information and wisdom from external, world-class experts and the elite advisors we work with about marketing and creating leverage
- ✓ All the "truths", tips, and tricks digital marketing companies in the financial services industry won't tell you
- ✓ Bonus content that you will get at the end of each chapter (they're called lead magnets!)
- ✓ Actionable insights at the end of each chapter that will allow you to start applying these lessons to your practice

The book will be broken up into two parts:

- **Part One** is about breaking down everything we know about the industry and digital marketing and rebuilding a stronger foundation for how your business tackles digital and creates a better future
- **Part Two** will dive deep into the individual aspects of building a magnetic, robust digital marketing funnel using The MAGNETIC Digital Advisor Model™

I want you to share *The Truth About Digital Marketing for Financial Advisors* with someone on your team who helps you with your marketing so that you can divide and conquer.

In fact, **if you share a post on social media about this book...**

Introduction

I'll send you a free copy to give to one of your teammates!

For the free copy, here's what I'll need:

- **An email** to Kristin@TriadPartners.com
- **Subject Line:** Truth About DM Post & Free Copy
- **Contents of Email:** Proof of your post about this book and a good mailing address

Finally, grab a pen and a notebook for all the ideas, opportunities, and questions that you uncover along the way.

While I cannot update this book every time there's a new story, breakthrough, or strategy, you can follow me for additional real time insights through my content on LinkedIn, Instagram, and Twitter.

LINKEDIN	INSTAGRAM	TWITTER
Kristin Shea, RICP®	@itskristinshea	@itskristinshea

I know many advisors operate with the weight of the world on their shoulders. This is not about giving you a bunch more ideas. Instead, the takeaways for your digital marketing will be proven and presented alongside scalable systems so that you are not just a better digital marketer, but a better CEO with more freedom in your life and business.

Get Excited. [1] ☺

---

[1]. *If you are a digital marketing company for financial advisors reading this and saying, "Who does this b*tch think she is?" I don't blame you. But keep reading and know that one of my biggest goals is changing an industry for the better. I'm not anti-marketing company. I'm pro-advisor, which I believe you are as well. None of my experiences or insights about "industry marketing companies" should be taken as blanket statements. There are a lot of you guys that I have a lot of love and respect for.*

PART ONE:

Deconstructing the
**Past and Present of
Digital Marketing for Advisors**
to Create the Foundation for
Your Ideal Future

Chapter 1

The Professional Hills I'm Willing to Die On

One advisor, Natalie, was focused on increasing and enhancing her firm's marketing to help generate appointments for her other advisors and increase her firm's growth trajectory.

Sounds like we're off to a great start, right? You would think so.

At the beginning of the year while meeting with other advisors at an event hosted by her Registered Investment Advisor (RIA), Natalie asked the CEO of an extremely successful practice if they had any advice on what she could do to ramp up her marketing.

Should she double down on something that's already working or introduce a new funnel? Natalie learned of a new marketing vendor who was serving that high-performing advisor's team up to 10 new leads a week.

Natalie was all over it. By the time her return flight home from the conference had landed, she had already scheduled an appointment with a company rep to learn more and get started.

She was in luck! There was availability in her territory at a relatively low cost of $250/lead with no additional front-end work from her marketing team. She too could gain 10 new leads a week. In fact, because of the area she was in, she was told that 10 leads a week would probably be on the low end.

Natalie was hyped. She had been wanting to incorporate more digital marketing into the firm's marketing efforts. The leads would supposedly be primed, qualified, and delivered with a bunch of background information—including net worth!—for her to call and close.

Sold.

Fast forward two months.

I get a call from Natalie. She starts with the good news:

"Kristin, I've almost doubled my lead flow since I started working with That Vendor. For the most part, their net worth is in the right range and they want help with retirement planning—my specialty!"

Definitely good news.

The bad news:

"But I've spent at least $30,000 over the past eight weeks on leads, and I basically have nothing to show for it."

Not good. Not the first time I've heard this.

It gets worse:

"And now my team is frustrated. We are struggling to get a hold of these people and often when we do, they just aren't who we thought they would be. The information doesn't match up."

We dug into it and broke down the process of how the marketing vendor created and delivered these leads. This is how it worked:

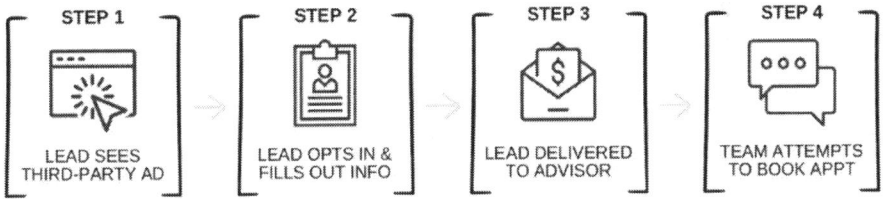

Step 1: Lead sees an advertisement created and branded by The Vendor while browsing the Internet or social media about taxes in retirement.

Step 2: Lead fills out their information and expresses interest in getting more information.

Step 3: The lead is immediately emailed over to Natalie along with any other info they may have provided.

Step 4: With the lead's contact info and background in hand, Natalie's team attempts to get the lead on the calendar for a first appointment.

I began asking questions:

"Can you tell me more about what kind of information you're getting about these leads?"

Usually net worth, age, gender, single/married, when they want to retire.

"Tell me about what happens when you contact the lead?"

Advisor calls and emails a couple of times and without receiving a response.

"Is the lead expecting a phone call or email from you?"

She isn't sure.

"When you call them, is this the first time they're learning of you and your firm, or is this vendor providing some kind of warm handoff?"

No warm handoff. While a couple leads recognized Natalie from receiving mailers for one of her dinner events, most did not know who she was or why she was calling.

"When you connect with them, how do the meetings go?"

They ask questions to learn more about the prospect's situation and go through their typical process, which speaks to their comprehensive planning system. They've had one or two leads become clients, but most of the people she'd managed to get on a live call said that "they have to think about it."

"Can you show me exactly what the advertisements look like?"

No.

I pushed back on this one and asked her to call The Vendor and report back to me with clarity on the advertisements generating the leads.

Two weeks later, Natalie came back with a handful of sample ads used to generate the leads that were now collecting dust in her customer relationship management (CRM) system. The content wasn't too far off from what the vendor had promised—it was branded by the vendor and related to general retirement preparedness. Each ad focused on a specific retirement topic and ranged from retirement income, taxes, health care, etc.

Ok. Got it.

So, I asked her what her goal was. What was her ideal outcome?

Natalie responded, "Well, I want to generate enough leads to keep my advisors' calendars full and we can bring on more clients."

This would be a great outcome, for sure. But it's incomplete.

While Natalie was absolutely right by knowing that she was providing tremendous value to her firm and team by filling their calendars…The approach was doomed from the start.

The *ideal* outcome and the basis for evaluating whether it made sense to hire the vendor and spend the money should have been *more specific*.

An example of a more specific outcome:

> "I want to increase the number of first appointments for my team and fill their calendars with <u>warm leads</u> who have a degree of <u>respect, admiration, and interest in my firm's approach</u> to building comprehensive plans <u>before they walk in the door</u>."

If we would have started with this more specific outcome in mind, alongside an understanding of where these "leads" were coming from, she admitted that she probably wouldn't have hired them. She would much rather spend her time serving people who are ready and excited to meet with her, versus chasing random people down.

The problems here, and lessons to be learned, are clear as day.

One of the big things we'll do in *The Truth About Digital Marketing for Financial Advisors* is what Natalie should've done from the beginning: <u>Work backwards.</u>

But first, what's happening in the industry that is setting advisors like Natalie up every day to fail?

Advisors, I'm going to shoot straight and speak from the heart here. I want to empower you with the knowledge that will help you truly evaluate what serves your business and what doesn't, so that you can allocate your time and resources to the things that *actually* make a difference.

If any of this chapter resonates with you, by the end of this book, you're going to walk away armed with the information and tools you need to create more meaningful outcomes at a lower cost and in less time.

But first, we gotta take the lipstick off the pig and get real about the four gigantic problems in the advisor marketing space and talk about some fundamental steps you can take to address them.

The reality is, many of the companies providing digital marketing services to advisors are:

1. Operating as a conveyor belt so advisors are confined to "territories" and forced to purchase one size fits all solutions
2. Choosing their own efficiency over advisor experience
3. Building a pricing model that ultimately overcharges advisors because they have to "do more" to compensate for lack of originality and viability, leading to lower brand equity for advisors like Natalie
4. Failing to align with the ideal outcome for the advisor first

Chapter 1

1. Truth Is...**The 2020 webinar rush showed us what we don't know about webinars.**

Anyone remember COVID?

When COVID hit, the biggest question for many advisors was this: "If I can't see anyone in person, how am I supposed to grow my business?"

That was a damn good question.

The answer came fairly quickly. Marketing companies quickly pivoted to a strategy that only a handful of advisors had already mastered with success: Webinars.

Does any of this ring a bell?

Any flashbacks to getting phone calls from every marketing company under the sun saying, "DON'T WORRY! WE'VE GOT IT!"

Were you one of the advisors who thought, "Wow, I'm NEVER doing seminars or in-person meetings EVER AGAIN and I'm moving to Fiji!" before your first webinar campaign even rolled out?

By the end of 2020, the general advisor sentiment on webinars was not good.

This quick pivot didn't turn out to be the game changer it was promised to be.

But it wasn't the webinars' faults. It's not that webinars don't *work*.

It was the mismanagement of expectations, lack of industry expertise, lack of advisor coaching, and misalignment.

Three things about the webinar rush astonished me:

One—How suddenly, everyone was a webinar expert.

Two—The cost of these new webinar solutions and how much more companies were charging above and beyond what it could—and should—cost to create the same results.

Three—How this "innovation" was still so far behind what world class experts in other industries had been using successfully for decades.

It was all a hugely rushed experiment, which is probably why the industry marketing companies landed at their price points and the product the price represented. How were *they* supposed to stay in business if live events were off the table?

The marketing reps seemed so confident, and I so badly wanted to see the promises come to fruition. But... Even as an eternal optimist who had to stay strong for my advisors, deep down, I was skeptical.

Webinars are a Money Maker…If You Do Them Right

At the time COVID hit, I had been working closely with advisors who had already been completely self-sufficient in their digital marketing for their events—both online and offline. And I couldn't help but wonder—is there a better way?

So, I hopped into the trenches and started helping advisors navigate the new webinar frontier. After a couple short months of simply studying and testing Facebook ads, I was successfully generating 30-40 registrations[3] for webinars at 25 percent of the cost that the marketing firms were charging advisors.

Some might refer to me as one of the "industry experts", but big picture, I wouldn't call myself a Facebook Ad genius. I just wanted to help.

But man... I was completely blown away by the results.

If I could create those kinds of results for the advisors I worked with, why were advisors paying thousands of dollars for a webinar with a couple of attendees that were created by the alleged "industry experts"?

Fast forward to today... Not only are webinars recognized as a viable marketing strategy for financial advisors, but our industry reaped many other amazing benefits from COVID that are here to stay.

Compliance took some steps into the future that made everyone's lives easier. We embraced and found value in virtual meetings, welcomed QR codes as a connection from real life to digital, and new worlds emerged as ways to bring on clients.

By now, we all know that webinars are not the same as live events. We also know that there IS room for webinars in our industry and that they do work. Unfortunately, during COVID when we were trying to wrap our heads around webinars, this was the reality of the situation:

Because we were collectively on our heels marketing-wise in addition to trying to figure out how to work from home with our spouse, how to get exercise with gyms closed, what was happening in the world...

---

3. *Registrations for an event, either in person or online, do not necessarily equate to qualified appointments and new clients. But, that's a different story.*

Advisors who were trying webinars weren't set up for success. Period.

For the one percent who were already digitally proficient in growing their business, COVID was no big deal. For those advisors, the brand-new webinar solutions being offered were not enticing because they could see them for what they were: A generic, untested experiment that was 10 years behind most other industries.

And for everyone else? There was a lot of time wasted and money flushed down the toilet.

I often hear: "Webinars just don't work."

They DO work!

They just must be done properly.

When the advertisements, the messaging, the format, the presentation, the call-to-action, the follow-ups are set up correctly and advisors understand how an optimized webinar works, they're a fantastic tool to have in your toolbox.

And that's what kills me.

It's not *just* about how the marketing companies over-promised and under-delivered on webinars.

The problem is, what happened with webinars in 2020 manifests every day.

Many Advisor Marketing Companies are Missing the Mark

Bottom line, many of the marketing companies in our industry that serve advisors keep getting bigger and bigger. The bigger these companies get, the more advisors they have an obligation to serve. When this is the case, advisors are left to mitigate two unintended consequences:

1. **The people at the top are getting farther and farther away from the end user, a.k.a. advisors.** They are too far away to listen to, understand, and market on the behalf of the advisors they serve. Instead, decisions about marketing offerings live and die by corporate spreadsheets evaluating opportunities for efficiency

2. **To deliver on the products they're offering advisors AND make money, they will do what's most efficient**—which is not always what's best for the advisor

It's not just the marketing vendors. You can observe this "do more, sell more, spend more" environment for advisor-facing companies in all corners of the industry.

And it's not just the webinars. It's the social media content, the emails, the events, the newsletters, and the websites.

All of it.

The outcome? Many of these marketing companies are choosing their own efficiency over your experience and outcomes.

> Tens of thousands of advisors are ALL using the *exact same content.*

Advisors using these plug-and-play systems think they're being good stewards to their companies and communities by using these tools, but opportunities slip through the cracks every day.

You cannot achieve your firm's digital marketing potential by leaning on overpriced solutions that aren't custom, innovative, or consistent with your unique approach to serving clients.

Especially when the solutions come from companies who aren't aligned with *your* ideal outcome.

I'm over it.

Chapter 1

2. Truth Is...In a virtual world, it's not good enough to be "the best" in your zip code.

If onboarding with your digital marketing partner requires a credit card for monthly billing vs a strategic and custom build out...I'm talking to you.

I'm *definitely* talking to you if your digital marketing vendor requires you to claim a "territory" so there's no overlap with other advisors.

Most marketing companies rely on templated, plug-and-play systems for every advisor they serve, creating an environment where advisors are limited to marketing in a specific geographic location/zip code to avoid marketing overlap.

Relying on your zip code or geographic region in this digital age is no longer an acceptable strategy. Consumers increasingly want to work with the best advisor **period**, not the best advisor in their *county*.

> Being the best in your zip code is not good enough anymore.

Michael Kitces, industry thought leader, keynote speaker, creator of the *Nerd's Eye View* blog at Kitces.com, and host of the *Financial Advisor Success Podcast*, shared a fantastic way to think about it:

"Imagine for the moment that you're coming back from the doctor, and the news is not good. *You have an extremely rare, potentially fatal disease. There may only be about half a dozen experts in the world who have even studied this disease and have any idea on how to treat you. Your doctor doesn't even know where to send you because they've never seen it before.*

So, the question becomes, with your life's stakes on the line: What will you do to find the expert who's going to save your life? You're NOT going to just ask your friends and family for a referral. You're going to go online to find the best person to solve your problem and save your life.

Patients and clients with simple problems stay local with friends and family referrals. The clients with the biggest problems, representing the biggest business opportunities, increasingly go online and say, "I've got a high stakes problem. I'm going to find the best expert to solve my problem. Geography doesn't matter when the stakes are this high."

If the system is so canned that there are geographic boundaries on where you can use it, how does that make your campaign the best?

Answer: *It doesn't.*

3. Truth Is...**You need to show up in your marketing.**

If you want to attract people to *you*, your messages and content must authentically reflect what makes you and your firm special and worth working with.

And no, adding your photo and bio to a boilerplate campaign does not make your campaign custom or help you stand out.

Most of the content being offered to advisors is designed for the masses. You know how that works—when you talk to everyone, you talk to no one.

Generic "stuff" cannot and will not create the outcomes you're looking for online because it will never create the trust and emotional connections in the same way that authentic stories and custom content will.

Chapter 1

Let's take this one step further.

What happens when you're using *several* conveyer-belt campaigns from *multiple* different companies?

Throwing a new company and their templated solution at each gap in your marketing funnel is the equivalent of creating a weird, digital marketing Frankenstein.

If you aren't familiar…The story of Frankenstein is about a monster unintentionally created by a well-intentioned man named Victor Frankenstein. After the passing of his mother, he was fascinated with the idea of creating human life. Victor spent two years meticulously collecting body parts with desirable features from mortuaries and graveyards. The goal of his science experiment was to create the perfect specimen and bring it to life.

Along the way, Victor realized that there were too many small nuances in the human body to create the perfect specimen, but he did his best. To navigate these complexities AND get the proportions right, he had to make his creature eight feet tall. When his creature came to life, not only were the proportions on point, but "he" had gorgeous, thick hair and brilliant white teeth.

Although it resembled a human being and the individual features were attractive (or at least as attractive as they could be considering they came from dead body parts), Victor was horrified. The pieces didn't match and had no life in them. Frankenstein was a monster.

This is what happens for advisors as they piece together their digital marketing strategy. I'm not saying that any advisors are out here creating *monsters*. But, when you're assembling generic, lifeless components from different companies…The pieces don't fit.

As excellent as the intentions may be, the collective marketing machine doesn't work. Or at least work as well as it could. There's no consistency.

And the more generic each piece is, the less authentically human your funnel becomes.

How can you expect the digital marketing equivalent of Frankenstein to be a game changer for your firm?

As Victor learned, there is nothing like the real thing.

You cannot outsource your firm's humanity and unique value proposition.

And *humanity* is a key word here.

As an advisor, you're probably familiar with the terms business to consumer (B2C) or business to business (B2B). You are also probably familiar with essential business truths, such as: *"People do business with people they know, like, and trust."*

With this in mind, I want you to throw the traditional B-2-Whatever out the window and replace it with a new acronym: Human to human, or H2H.

Chapter 1

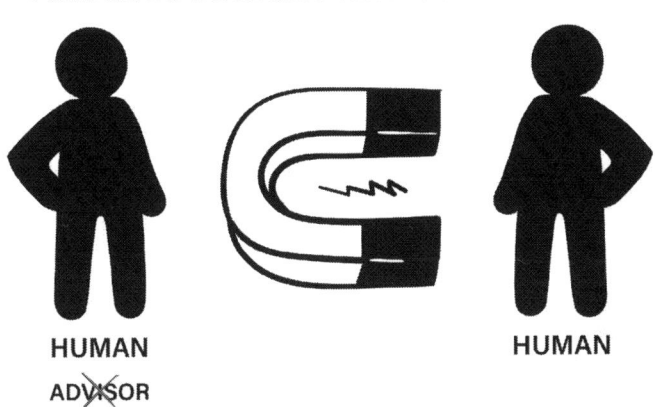

The "let's slap your logo and bio on it and call it a day" approach completely ignores the humanity and intimacy of the ENTIRE financial advisor-client relationship and process.

And if you want the human beings on the other side of the screen to show up, you'll need to do the same.

So…Are You Showing Up?

Kitces shared a story with me to help us understand how crazy it is for advisors to completely bow out of their digital marketing and fail to *show up.*

Imagine you're talking to another advisor who tells you that their new focus is networking with local accountants and business communities to develop their pipeline.

The advisor tells you they signed up for the local Chamber of Commerce meetings, but because they're "really, really busy," they hired a third-party marketing company to go to every Chamber meeting on their behalf to do the networking and pick up some referrals and clients.

How well do you think that's going to work out?

Do you think it's going to be nearly as effective as you going to the meeting yourself, telling your own story, sharing your expertise in your own words based on your actual experiences and passions?

Kitces doesn't think so. And I agree.

"Yes, you can have a third-party firm do a lot of background preparation and support in your marketing process, but if you send them to the Chamber of Commerce meeting and you never go yourself, no one's going to refer any clients," he said. **"You wouldn't dream of doing that in an in-person environment, but I see so many advisors doing it routinely in the digital realm."**

If you wouldn't do it in real life, why would you do it online? And why is everyone surprised when they don't see results?

And to bring it back to the Frankenstein concept—imagine having *different* individuals going to the same event week after week.

Advisors need to take Kitces' advice and start showing up in every single piece of their digital marketing efforts.

Marketing content created on a conveyor belt will <u>never</u> speak to the human on the other side of the screen in the same way that content from your heart will.

It is not enough to see your prospects and clients as humans first, assets second. They must FEEL it in every interaction with your practice.

> To earn someone's business today, you
> have to connect with their humanity.

Their vulnerabilities. Their issues. Their dreams.

They need to know you're a *real person*.

Not some random collection of generic, mismatching, irrelevant messages with abrupt (and sometimes aggressive) calls to action.

This is where the solution really starts and ends, and it's one of the most exciting opportunities in digital marketing. What it's all about.

If your campaign is built where a photo and bio swap is all that's required, it's a system built for the *vendor*, not the advisor.

You can't completely outsource marketing if you want to build trust and attract your ideal clients in a way that's consistently authentic to the heart and soul of your business.

And by using boilerplate content used by hundreds of other advisors, you're paying a price—in more ways than one.

4. Truth Is...**Advisors are spending too much money in the wrong places.**

While we're talking about prices...Too many financial advisors are unintentionally making uninformed, poor decisions about how to spend their marketing dollars.

Here's what I mean by that.

The marketing companies in the industry know that advisors need help. They know that most advisors are not digital marketing experts, and that they're willing to pay for solutions that "sound good" or seem "right" at surface level so they can check the box and move on to the next important thing.

I'm just not sure that advisors would continue to pay the price for what they're getting if they knew they could get the same results, if not better, at a fraction of the cost.

OR, if they knew they could spend the same amount on alternatives that creates a higher ROI that compounds year over year. We'll get to those alternatives later.

One of my partners in crime, Nick Whitaker, ran a successful financial advisory practice with his dad in Illinois before becoming a Business Development Coach at Triad Partners. He stays humble and wouldn't describe himself as an expert (spoiler alert: he's a marketing magician) but he admits he was perhaps a bit more curious than other advisors.

His curiosity led him to test his theory that there were ways to improve his ROI and results from his digital marketing efforts.

my partners & coaches in crime

What caused it? He was scrolling Facebook and saw **another advisor in the area running the exact same advertisements** for their events that he was for his.

YIKES. So much for territories?

Eventually, Nick became completely self-sufficient in his marketing and was no longer reliant on outside marketing companies to run ads, fill his educational events, or get appointments on the calendar.

By doing this, he not only experienced exponential growth in his firm's profitability but lowered his overall marketing costs by *50 percent*.

While major event marketing companies were charging $200 to $350 per registrant, Nick was generating registrants for between $10 to $100.

Clearly a discount, but what's interesting and important for advisors to realize is that this "discount" ranges.

"What a lot of people don't realize is how much the true cost to run a campaign can vary depending on the time of year that you're running ads," says Nick. "The same money spent will generate different results from month-to-month."

For example, in Nick's experience, November is particularly tricky to capture registrants—and ends up being the costliest time to do it—because you're competing with Black Friday ads from major retailers who also want to capture your ideal client's attention.

In November, he spent twice as much on ads compared to other months, like January, when it is a less retail-marketing-heavy season.

Even with the monthly fluctuations, when Nick started running his own campaigns, he was saving a ton of money over the course of a year. **In a bad month like November, he could still reduce his costs by about 60 percent compared to using a mail-house.**

And during a good month? Nick's firm saved up to **80 percent** of the cost per campaign.

Think about how these savings add up over time. What would that mean for your business?

Probably a lot. And he's not an anomaly.

 SETTING REALISTIC EXPECTATIONS: Costs of an ad campaign will also vary depending on other factors, such as your location.

Now here's the kicker.

> For all the money advisors are spending on outside vendors to build their pipeline, their *brand equity* should reflect it.

Instead, most of the time, this money enhances the third-party's brand equity more than their own.

And when the third-party service is turned off or discontinued, the advisor's firm doesn't have much long-term value in their branding to show for it.

Want to sell your practice one day?

The hundreds of thousands of dollars you may spend over the course of your career on third-party marketing will not be reflected in your firm's appraisal when it comes time to sell if it's all attached to third-party "brands."

Wouldn't you rather invest in your own brand than someone else's?

5. Truth Is...**You need internal and external alignment to see success with your marketing.**

There's a difference between the marketing company who can create results and the marketing company who can create results for *you*.

The key to getting results from your digital marketing is alignment.

Alignment in the way you build and fill your pipeline must occur at two levels:

1. *Internally:* Between the various pieces and people that make up the WHOLE marketing machine
2. *Externally:* Between you and the vendors or strategies you use

Internal and External Alignment

Alignment inside of your marketing machine ultimately allows you to show up with **consistency.** That consistency is the conduit to building greater trust in your marketing.

I'm not saying you need to bring all your marketing in house, but I do want you to think about the vendors you work with externally.

Most advisors use a different company for their website, their emails, social content, webinars, and events. Does that sound like you? If so, how much consistency is there between the content, messages, and offers?

Not much? That's an opportunity.

But here's the most important thing to recognize as you evaluate marketing vendors: Many of them are not aligned with the outcome that you're looking or paying for.

Not in some crazy, villainous way. It makes sense. But you still need to be aware.

The goal and revenue generator for many marketing companies is lead generation.

Your goal is converting those leads and growing your business.

LEAD GEN. ≠ LEAD CONVERSION

Too often, if marketing companies are generating leads, that's all they're doing. And then they're calling it a day.

Let's pause for a sec and talk about "leads."

I think the industry throws around the word "lead" too often and we've collectively lost sight of what a LEAD really is.

I tried to Google a definition of a lead that I was satisfied with, but most of them sounded something like this: *A lead is an individual or an organization who **"may" or "may not"** become a client one day.*

Oh. Okay?

Sit with that for a second. Like, lol, what?

Advisors have been sold so many "leads" at such a high price, that when these costly leads emerge from behind the lead gen company's velvet curtain, advisors expect way more for the leads than they get.

It's like, because we paid an arm and a leg for the "lead", we forget that **not all leads are created equal.**

Target the Masses and You Get the Masses

Typically, these leads are generated by completing some type of form or assessment from a third party and delivered to you, as well as up to two other advisors, for up to $350 a pop.

Sometimes, the lead just Googled a term related to money. For example, they may have looked up the definition of "annuity" because it was a hot topic at a dinner party amongst friends.

In no way does looking up a word related to finance mean someone is ready to hire a financial advisor. But that's how these leads work. You pay for a lot of unqualified and irrelevant leads.

Then, when a lead does fill in a form, you get a name, email address, phone number, maybe some information on where they are mentally and financially, and the marketing company can say they've done their job.

As they wipe their hands of the lead, your team now has the responsibility of calling those leads, chasing them down, and trying to get them to see the value of working with you.

But these leads—these *people*—have no idea who you are. And you might not even know how that lead was "generated" in the first place.

> Why are we chasing down people who might not even be prospects?

Get Your Audience to Chase You

Your ideal audience should be chasing YOU.

And if you come back to the lead gen company and say, "Hey, I can't get ahold of these people," you'll hear something like, *"We did our part. You need to get better at doing yours."*

No thanks.

There are too many great advisors questioning their worth because they can't convert these leads. This is wrong. It is NOT on you.

The inconsistency extends to seminar marketing and webinar marketing companies, too.

Many can and will fill the event... But do those attendees really matter if they aren't the ideal prospects for *you*?

At the end of the day, for each campaign or lead, regardless of the outcome, you're stuck with the bill.

This misalignment and lack of education for advisors is unacceptable.

If your firm wants to be the best online *and* offline, your efforts and investments should put you on the pedestal and boost your brand equity via a consistent message and value proposition from the top down.

Chapter 2

Funnels and Hurdles

Let's take our advisor and industry hat off for a sec and go macro on how digital marketing works and what the journey from *stranger on the Internet* to **client** should look like.

When we put ourselves in the shoes of our audience, it becomes very clear that most advisor marketing is ineffective because we are:

- Asking prospects to take the wrong action too soon
- Not understanding where prospects are coming from
- Creating confusion and distrust

Each of these will result in you getting ghosted.

In this chapter, I'm going to tell you an awesome—and kind of awkward—story about my husband and I that ties into the fact that:

1. Most of your audience is not ready to become a client
2. When we look at digital marketing as a funnel with three parts—a top, middle, and bottom—we can apply formulas that clarify the phases and motivators from top to bottom of funnel

3. Getting prospects from point A to B means priming them to make increasingly greater commitments as the relationship builds

This one chapter will change the way you look at digital marketing forever. And I'm hyped.

Digital Marketing is Not Like Dating

When Joe and I first met, I was 15-years-old, and he was an attractive, intimidating, and much older 19-year-old man with tattoos. I had a major crush on him. He just seemed way outside of my league.

We were in the same social circles and developed a friendship over the years. Not close friends, but friends.

At some point, he moved a few hours away to Richmond, Virginia to attend Virginia Commonwealth University. So, for about five years, we lived our lives separately. Did our college thing (or not-college-thing, in my case) until one day...

We matched on Tinder.

No one messaged the other. It was simply a Tinder match. BUT, a few months later, after a Friendsgiving, I saw Joe at a local bar from across the crowd.

I yelled his name at the top of my lungs—probably the tequila—and I got his attention; we caught up and exchanged phone numbers.

We were definitely, immediately a "thing." Dates here and there, dinner with his family, etc. I was super ready for the relationship, as I'd been established in my career for a while and, after all, he WAS my teenage dream guy.

Chapter 2

For a while, Joe wasn't as…Enthusiastic about the relationship as I was. Timing wasn't great. He was transitioning from college in a cool, hipster city to being back in his hometown, working a job in the government that he didn't love.

I know you're not here for relationship advice but, you can't water anyone else's grass until your own grass is watered. My lawn was green. At the time, his just wasn't.

It was a Sunday when I told Joe I loved him for the first time—a.k.a. dropped the "L-Bomb." He pretended he didn't hear me and asked me where I wanted to watch NFL Sunday football. Cool.

But also, understandable. Telling someone you love them is a lot like transferring your life savings to an advisor. There's no going back after you say it.

Although, we DO know that sometimes people say the L-word, transfer their money, and regret it. Cue things getting very awkward and messy.

But I had hope! Took him longer than I wanted, but after about four months of dating, Joe made it official by asking me to be his girlfriend.

Our love story as far as I'm concerned, officially began when Joe said I love you back, a whole nine months after I said it to him. Which, by the way, I said to him three times without him reciprocating. Not super fun at the time—it was extremely awkward LOL—but I knew we were meant to be.

I wasn't going to give up until I knew he felt the same.

Today, he's my husband and we live happily ever after.

Hopefully, you see where I'm going with this.

Turning a stranger into a client is a lot like dropping the L-Bomb because:

<u>One</u>—It's a clear, defining moment.

<u>Two</u>—You need to love every client you bring on and they need to love the possibilities you can create for them to live a better life and be the best they can be.

Chapter 2

In this story, when you have a prospect and audience that you *know* you can help and you want to work with, you're me. And they're some version of Joe on his journey from seeing the possibilities to having conviction to take the next step.

1. Truth Is...**Most of your audience is NOT READY to become a client.**

If you were to take a guess as to—out of 100 members of your ideal audience—how many of them are ready to pull the trigger and work with you, what would you say?

Maybe 50 percent? 20 percent?

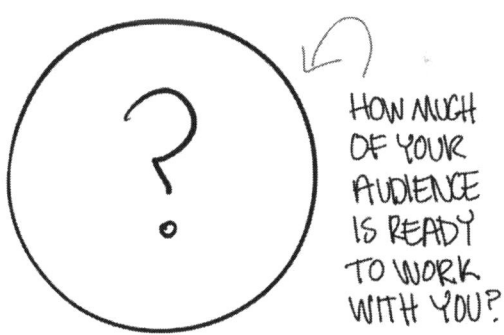

Go lower.

Only *3 percent* of your audience is ready to "buy" right this second. Whether it took nine months or five years to get there, at any time, there's about 3 percent that's ready to make a commitment.

The Reality of Your Audience's Readiness

According to the 3 percent rule, here's the full breakdown:

30 percent of your audience will probably never become a client.

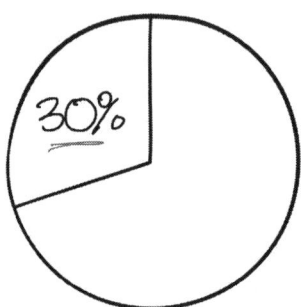

Not because you did anything wrong, but because it's just not in the cards. This can be the case for several reasons:

- They have an advisor they're extremely loyal to
- They have alternative options that work for them
- They're not in your niche. If that's the case, expect this 30 percent number to be bigger—and that's OKAY because disqualifying is just as important as qualifying!

> Forget about the people who don't align with your brand or offerings. And don't worry about catering to them in your marketing. *They're irrelevant.*

Another 30 percent will not be receptive to your offers to book an appointment because, while they may have an awareness of a need, they aren't in the market for what you're offering based on what's currently available to them or where they are in their life.

Chapter 2

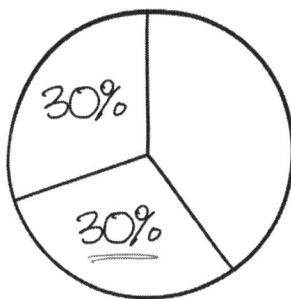

This is where Joe and I both were when we first met and when we matched on Tinder. The timing wasn't right and the idea of the timing *ever* being right wasn't on either of our radars.

A separate 30 percent of your audience knows they have a need for your services, but they aren't motivated to act on it. This segment can be tricky to read. Just like Joe was in the period between us exchanging phone numbers and him asking me to be his girlfriend. He saw potential but wasn't prepared to/was undecided about what to do about it.

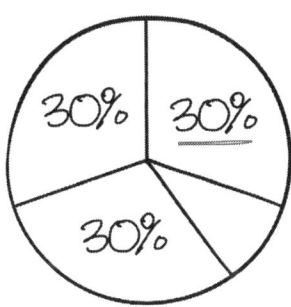

They are likely to engage with your content and send signals they're ready to work with you, but they aren't prepared to make a commitment. Yet.

The last 10 percent of your audience is broken up into two parts:

1. **7 percent** who can and will make a commitment and move forward but haven't yet. Usually this is because of a lack of information or having not found the right solution yet. Consider these people in the "research" or "consideration" phase. When you approach these people with the right value proposition at the right time, your firm can be the one that puts them over the edge. This was Joe just being Joe. He liked how things were going, but he wasn't sure yet that our relationship was "it".

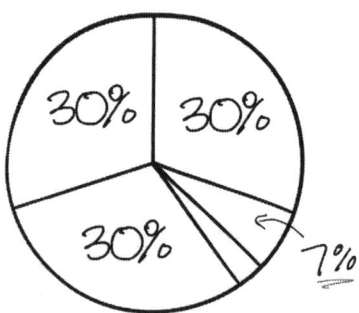

2. **3 percent** who are ready to buy. They're rearing to make a commitment in the next 30 to 90 days and actively searching for the right product or service.

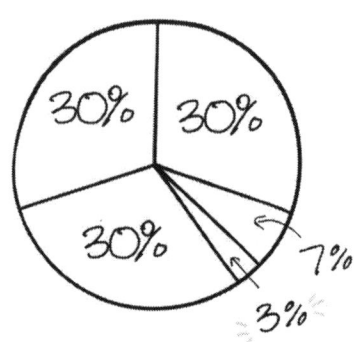

In your marketing—both online and offline: **IGNORE the 30 percent who will never work with you.**

For the rest? Make sure you've got a darn good funnel.

You will not succeed in your digital marketing without a true, comprehensive funnel. It is THE tool that guides strangers and prospects on the Internet to become paying clients. Any funnel framework used by world-class marketers, has three clear distinct parts: A top, middle, and bottom.

> Without segmentation between the top, middle, and bottom of your funnel, it's not a true funnel. *It's a sandpit.*

One of the things Kitces and I agreed on in our conversation about the digital marketing space was when he said, *"If you think of it in the classic three-layer segmentation—top of funnel, middle of funnel, bottom of funnel—**not many firms actually have all three parts."***

The industry's understanding of the three separate pieces of the funnel (or lack thereof) is fairly minimal—and therefore, a massive opportunity.

Now, let's talk about where your audience shows up in your funnel.

First, we will largely ignore the 60 percent of your audience that will never work with you or aren't anywhere near being in the market to work with an advisor.

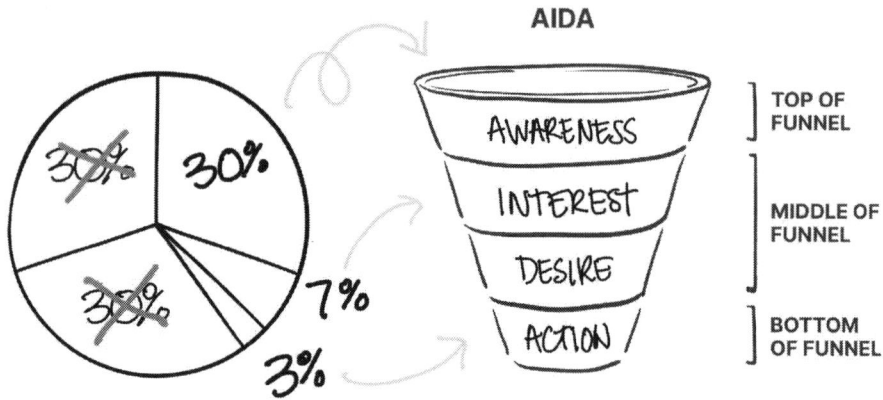

The remaining 40 percent of your audience will show up in different parts of your funnel:

- **The final 30 percent**—those who have an awareness of a problem but aren't motivated enough to make a commitment— will fall into the top of your funnel
- **The 7 percent** who are preparing to move forward with a solution will show up in the middle of your funnel
- **That tiny 3 percent** segment are exactly where you want them. At the bottom of your funnel

2. Truth Is...**You need a complete funnel using the AIDA model.**

Just like your audience has different objectives depending on where they are in your funnel, you should too.

Here's where The CAVE Conversion Formula™ comes in.

Chapter 2

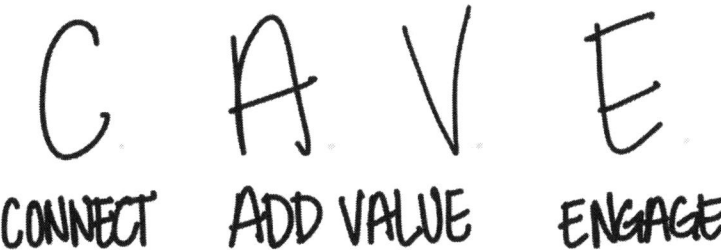

Top of Funnel Goal:
Connect & Create Awareness

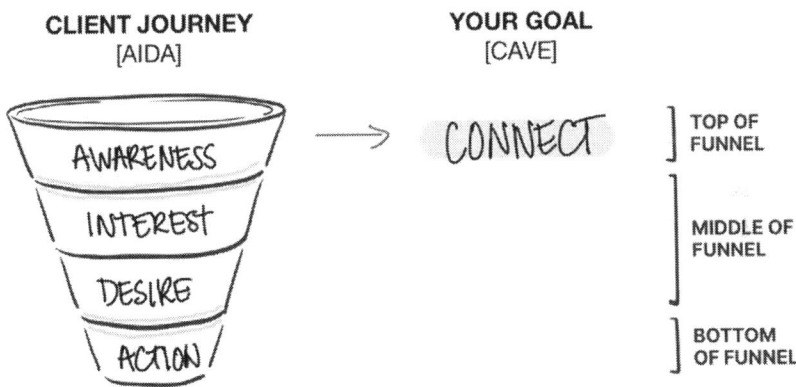

To connect at the top of the funnel means to show our ideal audience we exist and that we understand them, and create the **AWARENESS** that we can help them with the problem they need solved.

At the top of your funnel, you have the largest portion of your audience. They have an *awareness* of you what you're offering or an *awareness* that they might need some help.

Although they are not ready to make a commitment, we still need to talk to these people via a comprehensive marketing strategy.

Most of your audience today—even if your business is not using a 100 percent digital marketing strategy—is entering your funnel online, and that number will only increase.

Even if their first introduction to you is from a friend or a family member, they're looking you up on social media and then Googling you to find your website. They're evaluating several sources of content from the various ways you show up to find out what you're about and if you're legit.

Hopefully they like what they see.

To successfully connect at the top of the funnel, do these three things:

1. Introduce yourself to your audience with an emphasis on creating a connection between your firm's value proposition and heart and your ideal audience's ideal future
2. Bring people into your funnel by creating an awareness of who you are and the future or current problems you can help them solve
3. Make it easy for those with an awareness to move further into your funnel with an interest in having that problem solved or working with you

For those three primary objectives, focus on:

- Building trust and credibility by making it clear that you can add value
- Being consistent with your messaging across your various platforms
- Showing up authentically and creating an emotional connection with you and the humans at your firm

When building top of funnel content, keep in mind: <u>Every relationship begins with an introduction.</u>

And it NEVER starts with a social media post asking them to book an appointment with you because people *don't* go on social media to book appointments with advisors and hand over their life savings.

So, in every single piece of "top of funnel" content where you connect with new members of your audience, introduce yourself and boldly declare:

- Who you are
- Who you help
- What you believe in
- What you're known for
- What problems you can solve

Ask yourself: *What kind of awareness am I creating about how my firm can help my ideal client? And how easy do I make it for someone to take the next step?*

Often, you'll have no idea how many people are in the awareness phase because it's too early in the relationship for them to be waving any flags showing that they're paying attention.

But they're out there.

And if you aren't the one creating connections and awareness, another financial advisor is.

Middle of Funnel Goal:
Transform an Interest into a Desire by Adding Value

In addition to building on that initial connection and early relationship with your audience, you'll need to add value to your audience so those that have an **AWARENESS** of what it might mean to work with you build into an **INTEREST**, and then **DESIRE** to work with you.

Interest:

When the awareness phase is done correctly, some—not all—of that 30 percent who weren't receptive to working with you will develop an interest, which means paying attention to the problems you can help them solve and the value you offer.

Prospects in the interest phase are a little easier to spot.

General indicators of those in the Interest Phase include:

- Opening and clicking on your emails
- Engaging with your content
- Giving you their email address or contact information in exchange for a piece of value

The major thing that moves people from awareness to action and is at the core of the entire AIDA/CAVE Conversion Formula™, is the prospect's increasing urge to solve their problem.

Your content should be focused on reminding people of their emotional and financial pain points—but I want you to focus on empowering them to see the possibilities that become unlocked when their problems are addressed…Not scaring the crap out of them.

Focusing on building the trust and rapport that makes people feel like you're *the* person to partner with is done by: 1) Keeping it real and 2) Adding massive value.

Here's what someone thinks, for example, when they get an email from you:

"Is this good stuff? a.k.a., Is this person legit?"

"What are they trying to sell me?"

"Is there potential for this relationship?"

The best way to approach your audience early in your relationship is to give away 24-carat gold information and ask for nothing in return.

We'll talk about how to do this later.

Again, as time goes on, your audience's life changes—situations come up—and you consistently add value, you'll become top of mind. And that interest will develop into a desire.

Desire:

This is the smaller segment of those in the middle of your funnel who have developed a desire to solve their problem—and are actively considering their next steps.

General indicators of a prospect in the Desire Phase include:

- Signing up for more of your stuff
- Following you on several platforms
- Showing up at the event that they registered for
- Responding to your emails
- Asking questions and saying thank you

This is where that 7 percent of your audience who are preparing to make a commitment, but lack information and resources, come in.

Again: Rich, educational, and valuable content is what the middle of the funnel is all about.

Make a *conversation*, not necessarily a full-blown appointment, an option here, ie., putting something like *"Click here for a quick 15-minute conversation to get your questions answered"* on your website.

If you keep adding value, creating trust, and presenting no-brainer next steps, you won't have to push too hard to take the convo offline to a one-on-one setting.

They will do the rest on their own.

Bottom of Funnel Goal:
Engage & Make it Easy to Take Action

Prompt those with a desire to work with a financial advisor or those prepared to engage with your firm to **TAKE ACTION** on it—and make it easy to do so.

Your prospect *wants* to lock down a plan. They are shopping for their solution—not just window shopping—and are ready to make a commitment ASAP.

Even though it is a small group, this audience is *powerful*.

To get your audience to engage with you, you'll want to include:

- Personalized messages and videos
- Content and stories that represent successful case studies of other people just like them that you've helped
- Messaging that proactively reduce friction and creates a sense of safety via transparency and helps them visualize themselves taking the next step
- Prompts to take the conversation offline and set up a conversation or appointment using proactive, personal outreach and scheduling links

A lot of times, when you think of "building a digital marketing machine" you think you can automate all of it.

I'm going to show you how a lot of it can—and should—be automated.

But, for that small group of people who are ready and willing to *act* and make that commitment, personalization and a human touch is essential.

We'll talk more about personalization and the human touch a bit later, but first, let's spend some time going deeper on your offers throughout the funnel and what they tell you about where your audience is in their journey.

3. Truth Is...**You've gotta know the hurdles you're asking your prospects to jump over.**

Ever seen Leonardo DiCaprio's 2013 movie *The Wolf of Wall Street*? If not, it's worth a watch. It received five Academy Award Nominations, two Golden Globes, made me laugh until I cried, and is a great example of what NOT to do as a financial professional.

Fair warning, the movie set a Guinness World Record for most uses of profanity in a feature film. Viewer discretion advised.

The movie is based on the memoir of Jordan Belfort, a Wall Street stockbroker who started his career in financial services in 1987 selling penny stocks and ended it in 1999 as a convicted felon guilty of market manipulations and fraud.

After getting out of jail, becoming an international best-selling author and motivational speaker about business ethics, he has also taught millions of people his very simple approach to moving your audience: Straight Line Selling.

Obviously, I'm not saying we should ask ourselves how we can be more like Jordan Belfort (LOL), but, today, he seems to be using his masterful approach to sales to create a new living, and (I'd like to think) give back.

The basic idea is that any "sale" is a straight line. No matter how it could hypothetically unfold, there is a straight line and ideal path to get someone from point A to B.

Chapter 2

It's not A to Z. It's A to B, B to C, C to D, and so on.

Now here's where we add a twist.

When you think about getting someone from point A to point B, I want you to think of it along the scale of a 1-10.

Along this scale of 1-10, there are hurdles that your prospect has to jump over as they engage with you and move from a 1, a.k.a. not very primed, to a 10, a.k.a. ready to take action.

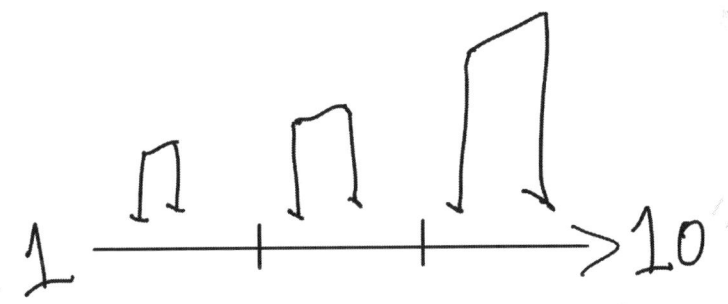

Those hurdles get bigger as they get closer to a ten. For simplicity's sake, we'll say there are three tiers of hurdles: *Low, Medium, and High.*

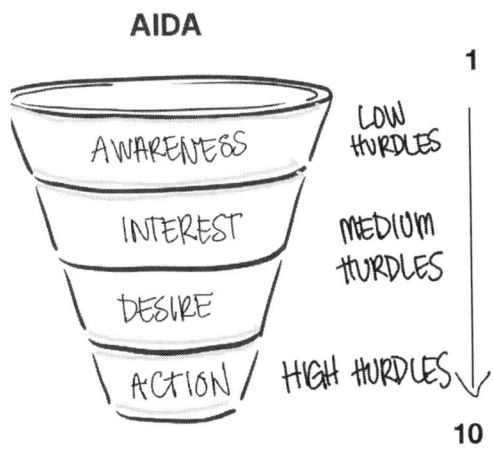

Those in the awareness phase would be a 1, a.k.a. not there yet.

If they're a 10, they're ready to take action, drop the L-Bomb, and move their money to join your firm's family.

Depending on where a prospect falls on this scale of 1–10, *think about your offers as hurdles.*

Because that's what they are for your audience. To access your offer— no matter how valuable it is—your audience has to be prepared to jump over some type of hurdle.

In other industries, the hurdles are usually price points. How much more is the customer willing to pay?

Let's say you want to renovate your home.

Downloading a guide about how to paint your new home is a low hurdle. The next, higher hurdle might be a pitch for a $200 consultation. If you follow through with the home walk-through and color consult, you'll be presented with an even higher hurdle, like $1,000 in exchange for a done-for-you paint job and home staging services.

For advisors, it's different.

Instead of being able to gauge how high the demand is for your ultimate offer based on how much someone is willing to pay for micro-commitments along the way, the hurdles for *your* potential clients are time, energy, and level of commitment.

 QUICK SIDE NOTE: One could make a case that you could pick up clients by starting small, taking what you can get, and asking for larger financial investments over the course of the relationship. But do you reaaaally want to build your business based on upsells? A.k.a., gathering a chunk of the portfolio at a time as you chip away at gaining their trust? Or would you rather build a comprehensive plan that involves capturing all the assets at once, with the expectation that all future assets uncovered will also come your way because 1) The trust is already there and 2) That's the point of having a plan?

Here are the questions they're asking themselves every time you present an offer:

Time:

How much time am I willing to invest in learning more about this person or hearing what they have to say? Would it be time well-spent, knowing that I have other commitments and that there are only so many hours in the day?

Energy:

Is this going to be difficult? Inconvenient? Is there other work I'll need or want to do in conjunction with whatever energy I've spent with you (like calling the Social Security Administration or digging out old statements)? And man, the day has already been so busy. Wouldn't it be easier to just rewatch *Game of Thrones*?

Commitment:

Do I even care about this? Is this an immediate threat to my livelihood or a problem I need to solve right this second? Am I prepared to take this seriously, or should I hold off until the house is on fire? Not trying have this random advisor blowing up my phone...

> These three main categories of online hurdles can be summarized by what I like to refer to as
> **TIA:** *Time, Information, Anonymity.*

At the top of your funnel, especially before there's a connection, your prospect won't be prepared to spend too much time with you, give you a whole lot of information, or put themselves in a situation where they have to talk to someone they're not ready to talk to.

Let's be real.

How many times a week do *you* say *"no"* to something, even if you really want to do it because you don't have the time or energy? Are you dishing out your email address and cell phone number to every person who asks for it online? When you do, how serious are you about actually talking to someone? Are you prepared to get a bunch of phone calls or texts?

I'm willing to bet that these are situations and decisions you face on the regular. I know it's true for me.

Put yourself in your audience's shoes.

Low Hurdles Are Still Hurdles

When your customer is not primed, go "low hurtle".

What I mean by that is, you're not asking them to make too big of a commitment or invest too much of their time or energy. You're shooting for **connection** and asking them for the bare minimum. You just want them to take the next step.

A few examples of low hurdles:

- Your website
- Social media content
- Easily to digest and access content (think quick downloads)
- Short-form, public videos
- General (not to be confused with generic*) communications
- Commentary or features in articles

- Blogs
- Podcasts
- Quizzes

But like I mentioned earlier, most of the time, you'll have no idea how many people are truly in this awareness phase. Not every marketing asset will deliver a lead, especially the ones with low hurdles to access.

And that's okay!

Remember, getting prospects to pay attention to you and consume your content—even if they don't give you their contact information—is still a win.

For example, a lot of advisors are lukewarm about their podcast efforts because the show isn't generating leads. Your podcast *should* be generating leads, and there are easy ways to do it, but **simply having someone new take the time to listen to your show is still awesome.**

Even when *you* see a podcast you do *really* want to listen to, there are still barriers that will stop you from listening. You see it at work. You start it in the car but get a call, so you pause it. Then you start it again, get home and the kids need to eat so you pause again.

Some people will get back to it and finish the show. And others, even though they really did want to listen to the whole thing, will never come back to it.

Every new listener makes a difference. Give yourself an extra pat on the back if a new listener sticks around for the whole show. If people are paying attention, you're ahead of the game. Take the wins.

And don't be so quick to declare failure and get down on yourself (or your awesome podcast, if you have one).

When you *do* you gather leads for those who aren't super primed, it's because you're using SIMPLE lead magnets and presenting an option to opt-in and gain value.

This will show up as your standard "lead" and lead capture.

You'll probably get a name, email, maybe phone number, and not much more.

Note, these leads are often the cheapest.

Are you putting the pieces together as to why I have no patience for the lead game and the insane markups on these leads?

One-third of your audience is currently here. That's a BIG representation. So, you need to have low hurtle opportunities to enter your funnel everywhere you show up online.

Warming Your Prospects for Middle of Funnel Hurdles

As a prospect moves to the middle of your funnel, they'll be ready for "medium hurdles".

The people jumping over medium hurdles are a part of the very tricky 30 percent who know that they have a problem that you can help them solve, will invest some time and energy into engaging with you, but aren't motivated enough to take *real* action.

These leads are a bit more expensive because creating a bigger hurdle means a greater investment of time and resources—for you and for them. This is easy to justify when the hurdles are built properly.

An example of a medium hurtle would be a webinar.

There's a bit more of a commitment for the prospect than just passing over their name and email because they're committing to spending some amount of time with you in a somewhat intimate setting, even if it's not one-on-one. They've gotta be okay with not being completely anonymous.

Those two things aside, it's not the hardest commitment for them to make because they aren't putting too much on the line. They aren't required to leave their house. They don't have to stop whatever else they're doing to focus on you (because who doesn't multitask when they're on a webinar?). And there's no face-to-face accountability.

But! They thought it was a good enough investment of their time to sign up *and* show up.

If they walked away from that webinar feeling like it was an excellent use of their time, you nailed it.

Other hurdles you'll want to consider throughout the middle of your funnel include:

- eBooks and other educational resources with more depth than an easy one-pager
- Offers that prompt them to give you their address so you can send them something in the mail (like a copy of your book or a bundle of notes from your top 10 podcast episodes)
- Webinars
- Custom email messages/sequences

The ask here is *not* to book an appointment. If you're making an ask, it's to begin a conversation or opt-in to offers that require them to spend more time and energy with you.

If you're adding big-time value and the connection is there, people will jump that hurdle.

Helping Prospects Scale Those Big Hurdles

We leave the "high hurdles" for the people who are ten-out-of-ten ready to work with you.

These leads tend to be more expensive leads, but long-term, they're worth it.

Now, one of the first things advisors want to do here is say, "Okay, let's just focus on that final 3 percent that is ready to go," but that's not the right way to look at this.

If you want to build genuine relationships with your audience, keep your pipeline full and create some digital relationship equity, your digital strategy must include hurdles that cater to individuals ranging all the way from 1 to 10.

Someone at a 1 is not a bad lead.

Let's say you run a campaign and generate 100 leads that opted in via bare minimum, low hurdles.

That's 100 new people to connect with! And the name of the game is NOT just identifying and closing the tens. It's constantly bringing in fresh new faces who naturally will need some time and TLC before they'll consider working with you.

Your goal is not only to be the person to plant the seed but *also* to be the person who maintains the top-of-mind awareness and guides them to solutions that are easy to act on when they're ready.

With that said, don't completely neglect that 3 percent that's ready to buy. If you're not asking, someone else is.

The ultimate hurdle is getting them to book—and show up for—an appointment with you.

Therefore, the content and strategies used here should be focused on personalization for the prospect and proactively helping them visualize working together.

These high hurdles and bottom of funnel nudges may include:

- FAQs
- Personalized videos, emails, texts
- Personal phone calls
- Case studies
- Managing expectations of what it would mean for them to engage with you (a.k.a. taking the pressure off)
- Offering ways to connect, like a 15-minute phone call, without committing to a full-blown appointment

Straight Line Sales—One Bite at a Time

The mechanics of an optimized funnel from a 30,000-foot view are both incredibly simple and, in a funny way, kind of overwhelming at the same time.

We're still talking about turning strangers on the Internet into raving clients and fans. And I know there are many of you reading this book who have yet to do this once, let alone consistently and reliably.

So, let's zoom out a bit. Take the pressure off.

You don't need to start looking at all the ones in your CRM and begin plotting all the hurdles you want to throw at them.

Instead, break it up.

Each component in your funnel and marketing activity has its own straight line from A to B. And B does not always mean becoming a client.

When you remember your goal is always to get them to the next logical step, you realize that each component of your funnel is a funnel in itself.

If they come across a social media post for the first time as a stranger, they're a 1. And as they jump over the hurdles inside of your top of funnel content, they'll eventually become a 10.

And you know what happens when they hit 10? They enter the middle of your funnel and become a 1 again.

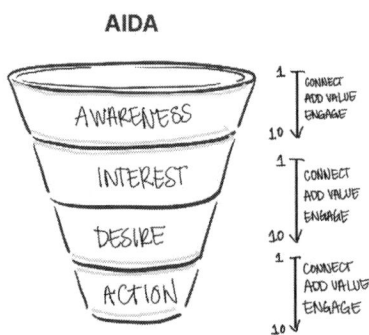

It's not just ONE straight line that brings people to becoming a client. Instead, it is a *series* of straight lines that build upon each other and ultimately lead to new client acquisition.

Having stacked paths to moving forward with you doesn't mean you're extending how long it takes to close someone. In fact, it does the opposite by providing you the clarity of exactly how you need to Connect, Add Value, and Engage (CAVE) so those with an awareness will one day take action.

Ever heard the term "funnel stacking"? Seem intimidating? Shouldn't be. Stacking next steps, a.k.a. what we just talked about, is really all it is.

Next Steps & Resources You Can Use *Today*

Grab a cheatsheet to identify where your marketing efforts may fit regarding AIDA & The CAVE Conversion Formula™ at: www.truthaboutdm.com/funneltools

Chapter 3

Vision

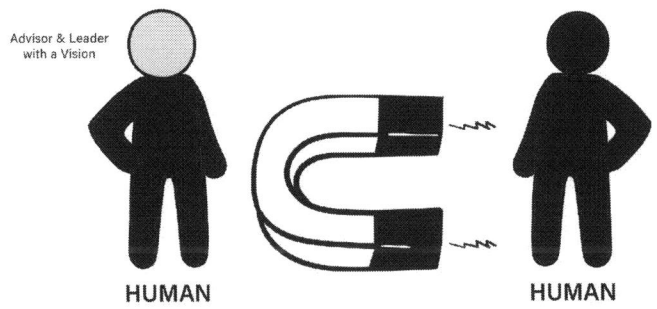

Let's put our advisor hat back on. Even better, let's put our CEO hat on.

Imagine that you're in medieval Europe, walking through a part of the country that's abandoned and underdeveloped, and you see three construction workers.

This construction in an untouched part of the country is intriguing.

What are they working on?

You walk up to the first worker and ask him, "What are you working on?"

He looks at you, confused that you'd even ask, and replies, *"Isn't it obvious?* **I'm laying bricks.**"

This answer doesn't satisfy you, so you ask the second worker the same question: "What are you guys up to here? What are you building?"

He replies similarly, and to be fair, the answer was fairly obvious: ***"I'm building a wall."***

Again, not satisfying. What is the wall for?

You ask the third and final worker. "What's happening here?"

Not only is his answer vastly different, but so is the body language that accompanies his response. With a smile on his face and a twinkle in his eye, he proclaims, ***"I am building the most beautiful cathedral in all of Europe."***

What's the difference between those three workers and their answers?

It's not that they weren't doing their job. They were all executing on their understanding of the tasks.

The difference is that the third had a *vision.*

Who do you think is being more purposeful in how they plan, set goals, prioritize, and manage resources?

The third.

The guy on a mission to build the most beautiful cathedral in Europe.

So often the way financial advisors, or even humans, try to set goals, create processes, and execute on new ideas is *completely backwards.*

Instead of asking yourself, "What's my ideal outcome?" we tend to ask, "What's my first step? Where do I start?"

I can't tell you how many times I've seen advisors chase new ideas, opportunities, and partners before asking themselves if it will support their ideal outcome. These ideal outcomes usually fall into one of three categories:

- ✓ More ideal clients
- ✓ A more efficient, profitable business
- ✓ Less time and stress

When you start with the end in mind, you can build a digital marketing machine that accomplishes all three at the same time.

Before we get to marketing, we must look at ourselves and our business.

Are we thinking about our marketing like an advisor? Or a CEO?

Good CEOs take inventory of where they are and where they've been to create a basis of comparison for where they want to be long-term. They craft a vision that clarifies exactly what this ideal future looks like. They inspire and attract others who aspire for the same type of future. And *everything* they do is part of a strategic, focused effort on bringing that future to life.

But the vision comes first.

This chapter is less about digital marketing tactics and more about the key to getting off the hamster wheel. We're going to lay the foundation for the rest of this book by priming you to think differently about how you approach your business.

Again, I'm not a fan of umbrella statements. But I believe advisors and their clients are being disadvantaged by the industry because there hasn't been a big enough emphasis on helping advisors be better CEOs and build better businesses. Hence our mission at Triad Partners.

The end goal of this chapter is to get you excited about the future and thinking like a visionary. We'll also create clarity around the role of digital marketing in your ideal future by learning:

1. How the evolution of technology has impacted marketing and your biggest obstacle going forward
2. Why you need to create a vision of your ideal future, versus looking at your feet as you sprint full speed ahead
3. How to think less like an advisor and more like a CEO to bring that vision to life via some great insights from a global business thought-leader

1. Truth Is...**You can't afford to think like a newspaper boy.**

A long time ago we had newspaper boys. Anyone remember newspapers?

They went door to door at 5 a.m. every day, delivering newspapers to subscribers. If they needed to get more customers, they would stand on the corners of every street shouting the latest headlines. This was one of the few ways available for people to get the news, and I can't imagine it was easy, but it got the job done.

And then, there was this brand-new invention called *the radio*.

People who lived in areas with good radio reception suddenly no longer needed to read the newspaper. They'd hear the news before it hit the printer.

The newspaper boys had to hustle harder to keep their sales up until the grind was no longer fruitful.

The print and news industries either adapted to and leveraged the new technology, or they were forced out and left behind.

Fast forward to 2022, and radio is battling to maintain relevance in the shadow of television and growing prominence of podcasts—a strategy that is *the definition* of meeting people where they are.

That's what the power of technology and the Internet boils down to: *The ability to meet people where they are.*

Do we know what the future looks like for technology and digital communication platforms? No.

But you can guarantee that every year that goes by, digital platforms will continue to get better, faster, and easier to use.

There will be companies that adapt and emerge in new markets. There will also be industry titans that fail and become irrelevant because they're too far behind to catch up.

If you're reading this, I'm assuming you're in the group that's not afraid of change and innovation. Cheers to you. Not every advisor is. This will serve you.

But it can't just be a thought. Being fearless in the face of change and failure has to be *engrained* in the fabric of your firm's culture.

I'll tell you from experience:

> Committing to *testing, failing fast, and failing often* is a part of the package if you want to be good—or even GREAT—at digital marketing.

And any advisor who is not proactively looking for ways to leverage the power of digital in their marketing is missing the boat. Period.

Too many advisors are approaching their digital marketing like the newspaper boy standing on the corner and stuck in the past as the world and technology passes him by.

At the mercy of his environment and "the man."

Screw that. Don't be the newspaper boy.

Get off the corner, stop waving that newspaper around, and think like the CEO of the radio company. And then, think bigger.

We do not have the benefit of being the only, convenient choice by default—like the newspaper boy in the heyday for printed news.

We are in one of the most difficult times to capture the attention of our ideal audience. And it will only get more difficult.

We Are Officially in The Attention Economy

If you've studied economics, you're familiar with the relationship between supply, demand, and scarcity.

Simply put, scarcity means that there isn't enough supply of a certain resource to fulfill an unlimited demand. This situation requires effective allocation of the limited supply to satisfy as much of the demand as possible.

This is the foundation of economics.

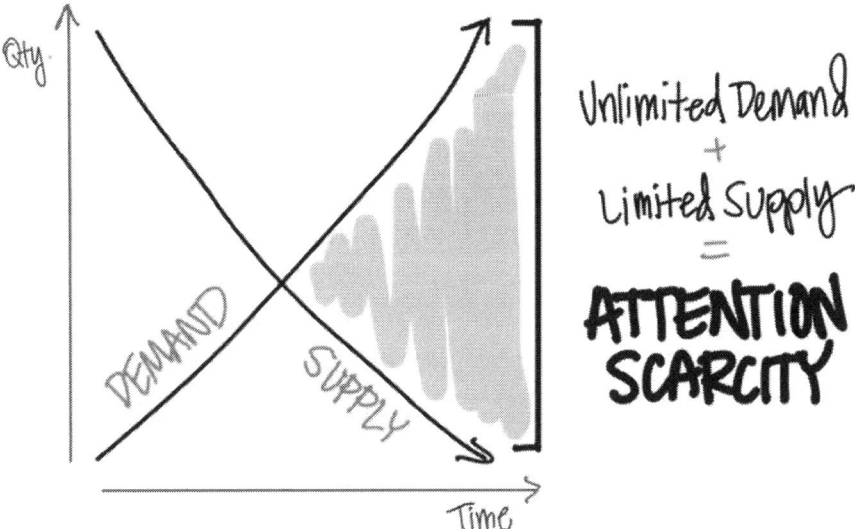

Usually when you think of scarcity, you think of something tangible.

Things like land, food, water, and housing. Essentials to civilization as we know it.

As technology develops and access to knowledge and resources increases, we face a different type of scarcity: Attention. Psychologist, economist, and Nobel Laureate Herbert A. Simon coined this scarcity issue as **"The Attention Economy"**.

We'll start with the definition of the word *attention*. According to the American Psychology Association, attention is *"a state in which cognitive resources are focused on certain aspects of the environment rather than on others."*

The first part of that definition that that stands out is the word *focus*—something that, on some days, feels like the ultimate pipe dream.

Anyone with an Internet connection has instant access to massive amounts of instantaneous information and stimuli.

How do we choose where to focus? Where to pay attention?

And then there's the second part of that definition worth noting—the fact that paying attention is a form of an exchange. When you pay attention to one thing, you're not paying attention to something else.

While our attention has always been both limited and valuable, today, our attention is arguably the scarcest resource there is. The thing with the highest demand.

Because guess what? **The money follows the attention.**

As we are bombarded with approximately 6,000 advertisements a day, our brains are on overdrive—looking for cues about what's worth paying attention to, and what can be filtered out.

Don't love it? Neither do your prospects.

You, as a financial advisor with a goal of creating opportunities online, are active participants in that war for attention. And I hate to break it to you but, just by being an advisor, you're an underdog in the Attention Economy.

I don't share this to intimidate you, but to give you serious pause.

> Getting people's attention is the hardest thing any business or marketer will do. Especially online.

What about who your firm is, or who you aspire your firm to be, is worth paying attention to?

2. Truth Is...**You can't win in the Attention Economy or achieve your ideal future without a vision.**

Most of the advisors trying to run a business haven't clearly defined *exactly* where they want to be in 3 to 5 years. Many barely know where they want to be from one week to the next.

So, of course, their team has no idea where *they* need to be.

They just take the tasks and the idea of the day and run with it.

Frustrating for you, for them, and a waste of everyone's time. Probably a waste of money, too.

How far are you gonna get if you're looking at your feet as you run full steam ahead?

Let's take a beat.

No more action.

No more projects.

No more tasks.

First, you need a long-term vision that you can align your capital, team, and relationships around.

So, What Is Vision?

Knowing what a vision is gets a lot easier when you know what it isn't.

A vision is not:

- × A motto
- × A tagline
- × A catchphrase
- × An external messaging strategy

The purpose of your vision is internal and ultimately illuminates the path of where you're headed for you, your team, and your partners.

However, this doesn't mean your vision is:

- × A plan
- × A process
- × A strategy
- × A method

Many people will confuse the concept of a mission statement with a vision. They are not the same thing.

Your mission statement is the "why". And your plans and processes are the "how".

The vision is the *"where."*

Where are you headed? Where do you *want* to be?

As a leader, having a vision means imagining a better future that currently doesn't exist, but is so inspirational, impactful, and worthy of creating that you are willing to commit to it today.

[**YOUR VISION & IDEAL FUTURE**]

aka, whatever you want it to be

It clearly describes where you are going. The destination. A vivid picture of where you'll be 3 to 5 years from now.

Here's another thing your vision is not: A single sentence. It should thoroughly paint a picture of what your ideal future looks like from all angles.

Big picture, if you're creating a vision on the behalf of your entire firm—not just your digital marketing—it includes the destination for every single aspect of your business.

It should be so clear, motivating, and inspiring that it's something other people want to be a part of and help you bring to life.

The vision doesn't stop or expire. Your vision will evolve as the years go by. Having a vision is simply knowing where you are going. It is not a place you will ever "arrive."

Your vision is living and breathing, just like you are.

After every year of actions and initiatives that support that better future, you'll come back and revisit your vision. NOW, what does the future look like?

Take it From a Vision Driven Leader

Earlier, I mentioned that you would gain insider information from world-class experts we've partnered with at Triad Partners. Allow me to introduce one of our strategic partners who provides intimate coaching with our advisors, Michael Hyatt.

Hyatt is internationally recognized for expertise in leadership and business development. Some of his accolades, aside from being the author of the bestseller *Vision Driven Leader*, include scaling a $250 million dollar publishing company, founding a business that is ranked year after year under Inc. 5000's fastest growing companies, and publishing several other books that have hit the bestseller lists for the *New York Times, Wall Street Journal,* and *USA Today.*

The access to Hyatt's insights has been an absolute gamechanger for the advisors we work with. I get absolutely schooled (in the best way) on every call he does with our advisors. If someone *outside* of Triad wanted to engage in a mastermind or one-on-one coaching relationship with Hyatt, they're paying between $20,000 to $100,000 (or more) a year.

On a quarterly coaching call with Hyatt and the founders of the firms we work with, Hyatt went deep on how to craft a vision that is not only inspiring for you and your team, but isn't intimidating to bring to life.

The mastermind call included a discussion about the four criteria you vision must hit before you and your team can align around it and execute:

- Is it clear?
- Is it practical?
- Does it inspire?
- Can you sell it?

When you have a vision of the future that checks all of these boxes, you can THEN begin to align your people and your plan and execute.

But the vision has to come first.

> *If you have a clear vision, you will eventually attract the right strategy. If you don't have a clear vision, no strategy will save you. -Michael Hyatt*

Mic. Dropped.

Chapter 3

Now buckle up for another great quote to inspire the way you think about vision. This time, from Whitesnake, a popular band in the eighties, in their banger *Here I Go Again*.

 LOL HI, DAD: My parents divorced at an early age, and I spent a lot of time in the car to and from his house for dinners and weekends. We listened to a lot of 80s music. It is what it is.

Check out the first verse:

> *"I don't know where I'm going,*
> *But I sure know where I've been.*
> *Hanging on the promises in songs of yesterday*
> *An' I've made up my mind, I ain't wasting no more time."*

I share this (very corny) quote with you to make a crucial point about another non-negotiable prerequisite for your vision.

You *cannot* decide on where you want to be in the future without taking inventory of where you've been and where you are today.

What have you tried and what are you currently doing?

What have you had success with? What do you want to do more of?

Where have you been, where are you today, and how does that shape where you want to be?

Your Vision for Digital Marketing

Putting the eighties music away and bringing it back to digital.

What does the vision for the future of your digital marketing look like based on your journey so far and the current landscape?

TOO MUCH OF ☹ THIS HAPPENING 	BUT WHAT IF? ☺
✗ Prospect is chased/bombarded	✓ Ideal clients seek you out
✗ Prospect has no idea who you are or what you want	✓ You're top of mind & they trust you're the right person to help them
✗ You aren't sure if the leads that come in are up your alley	✓ You proactively attract ideal clients & repel those who aren't
✗ Your team is spinning their wheels & wasting time	✓ Your team is celebrating inbound leads & appts on the calendar
✗ Long sales cycle, low close rate	✓ Short sales cycle, high close rate
✗ Lack of leverage via time in the day & human capital	✓ More leverage via technology, people, & processes

How Today Looks

You reach out to someone who knows nothing about you except that you are trying to sell them something. As their guard goes up, you put your target on a pedestal of sorts—*"Please don't hang up on me! Just give me a minute of your time! I have what you need!"*

If you're lucky, eventually you'll catch someone when the timing is right—when they have a problem that you can solve—and they're open to hearing about how you might solve it.

If you're diligent *and* organized *and* have a consistent, strategic cadence, you'll eventually earn an opportunity to engage in a dialogue.

But how many people are diligent or organized or manage their time well enough to make the 8 to 15 touches necessary to earn their attention?

Not many.

Is there merit in playing the numbers game and blasting your value proposition with a wide net? Sure. For some.

But...I'm going to take the strong stance that "spraying and praying" is NOT a strategy. It's a lame and inefficient way to do business. *Not* "ideal future worthy."

When you run your business like it's 1995—there are only so many people you can see or call or talk to in a day.

What Tomorrow Looks Like...With Vision

Imagine an alternative where your ideal prospects are reaching out to you because you have created a connection and earned trust from afar.

Where they're hand delivering their problem in gold wrapping paper because they already know you can solve it.

Where the sales cycle is half the time because they were "sold" before they even contacted you.

Where *you're* the one on the pedestal?

It won't happen on its own.

You will not drift your way to being the exception.

Where are you trying to go? And what does that have to do with your digital marketing in the Attention Economy?

Everything.

3. Truth Is...**You gotta zoom out and double down.**

I can't dictate your ideal future. You might not be able to describe it right this second either. And that's okay.

I have no interest in pushing you toward one platform or another. The marketing companies do enough of that. ;)

What I *will* do is give you some guidance on how to land on a destination you'll have the passion and endurance to commit to long-term by considering these three things:

1. Authenticity
2. Consistency
3. Focusing on the "WHERE" over the "HOW"

Authenticity: Start within yourself and what is authentic to you.

Working with the end in mind means knowing exactly who you and your firm represents and being radically clear about what that means from start to finish and from the inside out.

When you know exactly who you are and where you're going, you create a secret weapon for your firm in a highly commoditized market because you know exactly who you are (and who you're not). When exploring a new opportunity, the question is simple: "Does this align with who I am and want to be?"

If the answer is "no"—no matter how shiny the object is—it's a no-go.

While I have no interest in dictating your future, I strongly encourage you to consider the power of bold, radical authenticity. **Authentic alignment from the inside-out is the only way to ensure your efforts to bring your vision to life are sustainable.**

For some, committing long-term to going all in on what makes you human comes naturally.

For others, it takes courage.

For most, it takes a lightbulb moment, or series of lightbulb moments, to truly understand how much you're leaving on the table by choosing a future that is palatable for the masses as opposed to authentic to you and magnetic for your firm.

The Day It Clicked

My big Authenticity Lightbulb Moment happened in the infancy of my LinkedIn journey when I shared a raw, emotionally charged video that I regretted posting the second I shared it.

The day before I shared the video, a younger female colleague approached me, distraught and searching for advice.

A male advisor she was prospecting had crossed the professional line and made her extremely uncomfortable in an in-person setting.

"Has this ever happened to you?" she asked me. "What should I do?"

Of course, I'd experienced something similar.

I still do sometimes.

But I didn't know what to tell her.

Establishing boundaries and removing yourself from the situation is sometimes impossible to do. Plus, I knew her question was bigger than the isolated incident.

I reluctantly told her that as a young female in the business, she would essentially need to learn how to deal with it.

I thought about my response on the drive home from work, the entire evening, and woke up the next morning thinking about it, increasingly frustrated and disappointed.

After a long drive to work the next morning with this conversation still on my mind, I pulled out the camera on my phone, not thinking twice about how unprofessional I might look in my leather jacket or with damp hair from that morning's shower and recorded a video.

In it, I shared a story about a the situation I had walked away from mortified, questioning my worth and value, and ultimately just had to "deal with it."

Long story short, about a year prior, I was at an event with about 30 leaders in the annuity distribution space. I was the only female in the room and the youngest in the group.

After the day's meetings, we headed to the hotel bar to have a drink as a group and play a trivia game.

During the game, a question came up, prompting players to "name a hole you can't get into."

One guy, a leader of the group in both seniority and stature, and a "peer" of mine, pointed at me, in front of the entire group, and said, *"Like this one?"*

……..??

He literally called me a HOLE he couldn't get into.

I was stunned.

I paused, asked him to repeat himself, which he didn't, and everyone moved on.

Chapter 3

But the damage was done. No bueno.

Caught up in the emotions of reliving this moment, I didn't think through the video or how "aggressive" the story was. I just hit the record button, spoke from the heart, and immediately uploaded to LinkedIn.

No more than three Mississippi's after I hit "post," the panic set in.

"Why did I do that? What if advisors see that and don't want to work with me anymore?"

Me second-guessing whether I'd make a mistake didn't last long. That post became the foundation and catalyst for my success online.

Here's what happens when you get real: The people who can identify with you on a deep level are going to feel so much more connected to you. Those who don't? You probably don't want to work with them, anyway.

Any advisor who watched that video and thought that the comment I received was a non-issue or that my frustrations were invalid is someone I *do not* want to work with.

Meanwhile, I received a flurry of comments and messages, not just from other women, but also men(!) inside my target audience. Sharing their experiences. Thanking me. Promising that if we were to work together, they would never cross that boundary.

Cue the lightbulb moment: My radically authentic message resonated with my ideal audience and opened doors to create my ideal outcomes.

I'm *not* saying that you should try to be controversial to capture people's attention.

What I will say is this:

Censoring yourself and your firm's truth for the sake of being palatable for the masses *does not serve* you the same way that keeping it real does.

If you don't believe me, what if I told you that a video I posted about this story accumulated almost 20,000 views and 500+ reactions from my audience?

Imagine how magnetic you become when this level of authenticity exudes in every interaction with your firm because it is a guiding force for your business.

Does your firm exude what's authentic to you? If not, that's okay. It can, and will, one day, if it's intentionally a part of your vision.

What is your firm's truth?

No Consistency, No Results

A vision isn't something that talks about next month's or next quarter's goals. This is your long-term future. If you cannot commit to this ideal future in 3 to 5 years, it should not be a part of your vision. Following through on this long-term plan requires consistency.

Although your vision is meant to be an internal guide, it has external benefits. When you create something you can be consistent with internally, you will be more consistent externally.

In every single way that you, your firm, and your value proposition show up (both online and offline), you gotta be consistent.

If you are not consistent with your messaging, offers, and interactions from day one, you will do one of two things, and sometimes both:

1. CONFUSE your clients
2. Make it difficult to build trust

Chapter 3

On a micro level, I see advisors make this mistake every day by focusing on too many problems instead of one *specific* problem that they're really great at solving, or an outcome they can help create.

I get it. You can do so many important things for your clients and prospects.

Investments, tax planning, college planning, risk management, insurance, retirement income, accumulation planning...The opportunities are endless.

But, to get people feel confident in moving forward with you at any level, **you have to be consistent** with the problem you can help them solve or the outcome you can help them create.

When you're talking about a problem you can help solve one day and then a different problem the next, you'll confuse/overwhelm them and slow your conversion rates.

Here's an example. A prospect, who may have developed the intention to get your help achieving their legacy goals after watching your video series about transferring wealth will be sent back to square one when you take a hard pivot to go super deep on Roth Conversions.

When you have a clear vision for your ideal client and how you help them, you'll find that the emphasis shouldn't be on the individual pieces of the financial puzzle, but instead the comprehensive outcome and destination.

When your value proposition is specific and consistent, the path from stranger online to raving client is much faster—for all parties.

You can't stick to a story or narrative long-term if you haven't established one.

Focus on the "Where", not the "How"

You can't bring your vision to life if you don't have one. But you won't be able to create the meaningful and inspiring future that *deserves* to exist if you're bogged down by the "how."

If you focus too much on the "how" while you craft your vision, you're limiting yourself to creating a future based on your understanding of what's currently possible.

The vision assumes that *anything* is possible.

Figuring out how you're going to get there comes afterward.

Compliance: The elephant in the room

I know people who have been burned, dejected, and uninspired to pave new paths in their marketing based on roadblocks constructed by compliance. They won't be able to wrap their heads around crafting a vision that addresses the "how" after the fact without knowing, *"What about compliance?"*

Let's address this here and now.

For every advisor who has had compliance take the wind out of their sails, left them feeling stuck, or has made them uninterested in exploring future possibilities after years of being shut down—I FEEL FOR YOU.

Chapter 3

It's heartbreaking to be shut down on an exciting opportunity you've invested in. It's even worse when you hear "no" more than you hear "yes."

If you have a compliance team that just doesn't understand or give you a lot of freedom to leverage the power of digital marketing, it might be time to reconsider your setup.

I know that's a massive lift. And a big change for both your team and your clients.

However, you do still have choices if you can't change your firm set up or compliance team.

And it begins with mindset.

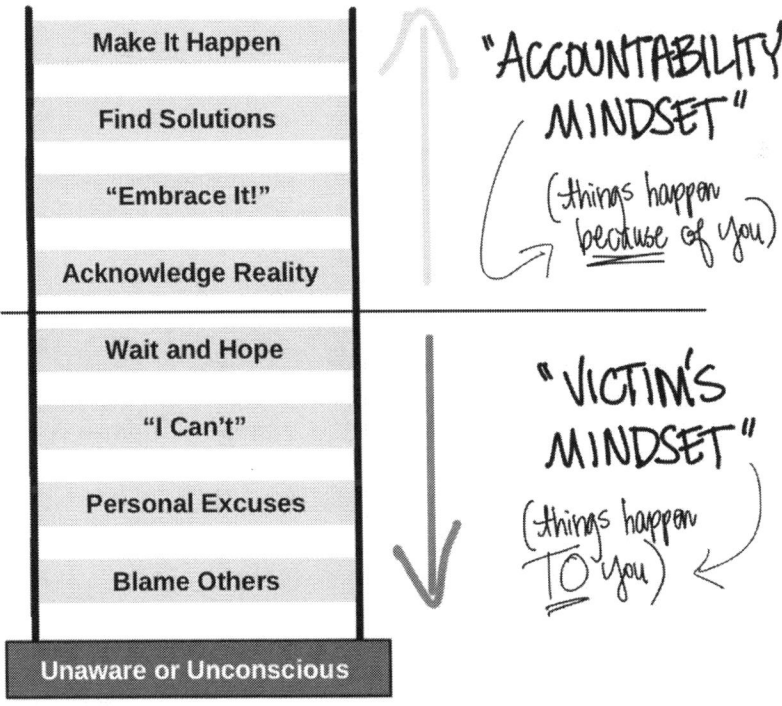

There are so many things that compliance doesn't have control over.

- They don't tell you that you can't have a niche
- They don't dictate how many marketing funnels you can have
- They aren't going to tell you that you can't use digital funnels
- They don't require you to use stock images
- They don't tell you not to use calls to action
- They don't control the quality of your videos

Finally, they don't control who you are and what makes your firm special.

We'll get to this later, but the *best* content is going to be the content that is most personal to you, your story, and your voice.

Here's the deal:

> Those who focus on *what they can control* create better outcomes.

The advisors who are crushing it online are proactively deciding to navigate and improve their situation based on the things they can control.

And they aren't thinking about all the ways compliance may impact their ability to create a better future.

Will there be other roadblocks? Of course. **Congratulations on being human.**

What you'll find when you have a clear and inspirational vision for your firm—marketing included—is that, when the going gets tough, your vision reminds you that every roadblock you hit isn't really that bad. The destination will be well worth it.

Chapter 3

Next Steps & Resources You Can Use *Today:*

Listen to a conversation between Daniel Crosby and I on his podcast *Standard Deviations* for six psychological hacks to standing out in The Attention Economy: www.truthaboutdm.com/attentioneconomy

Chapter 4

Your Magnetic, Authentic Brand

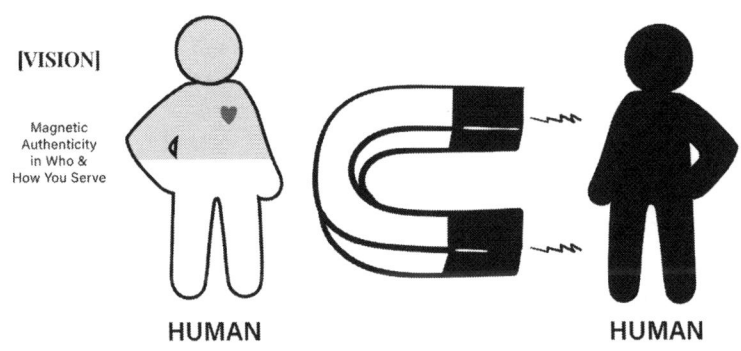

Advisors are in one of the most commoditized industries on the planet.

Here's a quick definition check to make sure we're on the same page about what that means.

A commodity is a basic good that is interchangeable with other goods of the same type. While the quality of any given commodity may slightly differ, it is essentially uniform across producers.

> How are you supposed to show up in your marketing as the superior choice in a sea of same-ness?

For the most part, advisors use a similar set of tools, products, and strategies to work with clients. And ultimately, the value proposition and ideal client is often interchangeable from one firm to the next.

Don't agree? Most investors do.

In a study done in 2018 by BNP Pershing, 63 percent of investors agreed with the statement, *"All financial advisors make the same promises, making it difficult to distinguish between one and the next."*

People simply cannot tell advisors apart.

Due to a lack of standardization industry wide, advisors have all the freedom in the world to shake things up and think outside-of-the-box.

But most don't. And it kind of bums me out.

You can do, be, and show up however the heck you want!

And I hate to break it to you, but I bet if you pull up your website and compare it to another advisor's, the messaging is similar.

Here's the thing about marketing:

Your marketing should be a magnet. Yes, magnets attract. But they also *repel*.

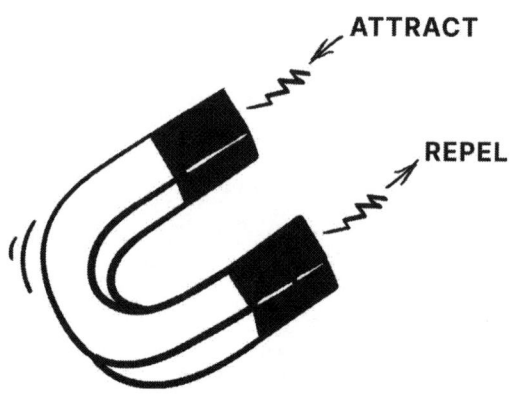

Chapter 4

And you can't do either—or grab too much attention—without *de-commoditizing* your marketing efforts by*:*

- → Defining exactly who you are
- → Dialing in your audience
- → Simplifying and packaging your value proposition

1. Truth Is...**McDonald's De-Commoditized like a boss.**

Accepting that most of your audience can't tell what makes an advisor special is a tough pill to swallow, so let's imagine that we are operating inside a different, highly commoditized industry: Fast Food.

From there, let's shine a spotlight on one of the first restaurants (if we want to call it that) that not only differentiated itself, but did so in a way that was duplicatable: McDonald's.

Mack and Richard McDonald were two brothers from New Hampshire who made a move to California with their eyes set on Hollywood—an industry they were ultimately unable to break into.

Funny enough, like most financial advisors and myself, the McDonalds brothers unintentionally stumbled into their career. During a stint at a theater managing concessions, Mack and Richard discovered their passion for the food and service industry.

They opened the doors to the first McDonald's in San Bernadino, California in 1940.

When McDonald's first opened, it was a ribs restaurant that ran a similar service model to most of the restaurants at the time—a drive-in.

Cars would pull up and carhops, a.k.a. young women on roller skates, would provide kitchen to driver seat service. Indoor dining was not an option.

Despite their early success, Mack and Richard saw room for improvement. The changes they made were the first steps to transforming the entire industry forever.

How to Differentiate as a Commodity

Did the drive-in model work? Yes.

But, to the disdain of Mack and Richard, the carhops attracted teenage boys who would loiter and overstay their welcome. They were afraid that their ideal customers—middle class families and the working class—were put off by these distracting spectators.

How could they solve it?

By eliminating the drive-in method and switching to a self-service model.

In 1948, after shutting down for three months, McDonald's reopened and introduced its new *Speedee Service System*. We'll talk more about this system in the next chapter, but the shift to self-service and away from carhops replaced loitering teenage boys with more paying customers in their ideal demographic.

Bonus points for Mack and Richard: By eliminating the staff required to serve the customers in their cars, they not only increased profits with more paying customers, but they lowered their business expenses and costs of labor.

This was the first step towards the drive-thrus we know and use today—not only in fast food chains, but when we want to get a latte from Starbucks or access our bank account on the go.

Well done, guys.

Focus: You Are Not All Things to All People

As mentioned above, and to the surprise of most—me included—McDonald's began as a full-service restaurant with a specialization in BBQ ribs.

Around the same time McDonald's made the switch to cashiers and self-service, they made another drastic change. Richard and Mack decided to focus on their best-sellers and whittled the menu down to a whopping nine items. To the dismay of many, ribs were one of the items cut.

They basically said, "This is it, guys. Take it or leave it."

Could they have kept the other items on their menu to avoid repelling those who came for the ribs?

Sure.

But they were a mission for maximum operational efficiency.

Richard told *The Chicago Tribune* in 1985, "You make a point of offering a choice and you're dead. The speed is gone."

We'll talk more about the relationship between speed and costs later, but as McDonalds' speed went up, their costs went down. And revenue immediately sky rocketed.

Before eliminating the car hop model and streamlining the menu, they made $200,000 a year in sales. After those two adjustments, sales revenue increased to $300,000 and expenses decreased by a third.

Adjust the value of the dollar in 1948 to 2022 and you realize that's more than a $1.2 million dollar boost in revenue. In one year.

Differentiate, Differentiate, Differentiate

If you want to get a hamburger with two patties, or a double-decker hamburger, you can go anywhere.

Two patties, lettuce, tomato, pickles, ketchup, and onion. The components of a double-decker hamburger are pretty universal.

But there is only one place where you can get a Big Mac.

McDonald's.

Is it any different than any other double-decker hamburger out there?

Sure. The individual parts and ingredients—meaning the buns and everything in between—are not the same ingredients as the restaurants' down the street. Plus, McDonald's added a *special sauce*. So, no, not all double-decker hamburgers are the same.

But when you eat a double-decker hamburger, do you choose the restaurant based on color of the tomato on the burger? Number of seeds on the bun? No. You buy the whole package. You want the two patties and if you're not a fan of pickles, you'll have them take them off. No big deal.

McDonald's did not change the definition of a double-decker hamburger.

What they DID do was de-commoditize by *packaging* a commoditized product and create something completely proprietary to McDonald's... while staying true to an efficient, focused business model and menu.

If you want to get a Big Mac, you go to McDonald's. Period.

Let People Know You're Unique

I talk to advisors every day who have amazing stories, missions, and teams. Making connections and hearing each advisor's unique journey is my favorite thing about what I do.

The *services* are commoditized, but I have never met two advisors who are the exact same.

This may sound harsh but, there's no value in being unique if nobody knows that you are.

> You cannot assume that people know exactly why you aren't *"just another advisor"* if you cannot clearly articulate it.

You must be able to clearly articulate and boldly declare it over and over anywhere you show up.

Attention spans are short, remember?

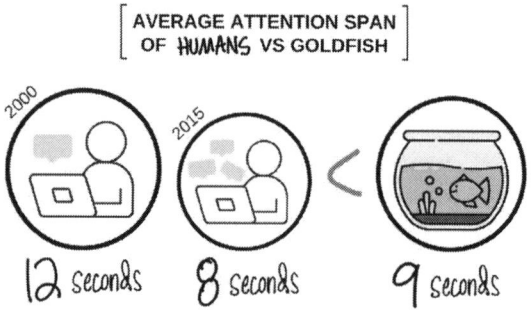

Your digital marketing will forever be way harder than it needs to be if you do not de-commoditize.

Of all the questions to consider regarding where you're headed, these three are arguably the most important:

1. Who do you serve?
2. What do you do that's unique and means something to them?
3. How is your value proposition packaged in a way that captures attention?

Chapter 4

End goal in one of the most commoditized industries on the planet? A magnetic, authentic brand. Assuming that's part of your vision.

2. Truth Is...**You have to ask yourself "who?" not "how?"**

I hear the following question all the time: "Where do I start if I want to use digital marketing in my firm?"

I always respond with the following question: "Who is your ideal client?"

Consider an important concept from one of Dan Sullivan's most popular books *Who? Not, How?*

Basically, when you focus on the "WHO", the "HOW" will take care of itself.

Most advisors haven't really defined the "who".

Truth is, Adam crushed this.

Allow me to introduce Adam Cmelja. Adam's marketing strategy turned 2020 into an insanely successful year.

Adam is the preeminent advisor for optometrists. But it wasn't always this way.

Initially, Adam's "niche" strategy was working with doctors. In 2018, he dialed it in deeper and focused his efforts on one specific corner of the medical professionals' universe: Optometrists.

Although 99.99 percent of the population would not find Adam's value proposition relevant, he's seen firsthand that the clients that *do* are no small fish. Each one represents a minimum of $12,000 to $13,000 in annual fees.

The Truth About Digital Marketing for Financial Advisors

So how did he get there?

2018 is what Adam would tell you was his "ramp up" period. As he dialed in his audience, and crafted messages/brand assets accordingly, he kept the following question in the front of his mind:

"How can I take what I know and put it through the filter of what they understand?"

2019 was spent drinking out of the fire hose by putting himself in his audience's shoes and learning everything he could about their biggest problems and how to solve them. From there, he began crafting a brand, messaging, and campaigns catered to those unique needs and offerings.

A great example of this would be Adam's website. Visitors are not greeted by the basic stock images of pre-retirees on a sailboat, but an enormous image of eyeglasses and a strong headline telling his audience that he can help them *see the world more clearly*.

Every single part of how Adam shows up is a dog whistle to his ideal audience.

In 2020, Adam says "the dam broke."

 QUICK SIDE NOTE: Remember how we talked about how your vision should be three to five years out? Love the parallel here and how this played out for Adam in a similar timeframe.

He started the year by relaunching his podcast with a new name and mission. *20/20 Money* allowed him to speak directly to the people was trying to target.

And then, COVID happened.

Chapter 4

While most advisors were running generic campaigns about the COVID economy and providing brief overviews of the Paycheck Protection Program (PPP) alongside other corresponding economic updates, Adam's team got super specific.

Many eye doctors running independent practices faced obstacles that many small business owners could've also related to: Not being able to serve people virtually, not being able to have patients come in, struggling with keeping their staff employed.

But Adam wasn't targeting business owners.

Because of his dialed-in approach to optometrists, his messages catered to their exact pain points, and he stood out from the crowd.

Remember: The future of how people choose their financial advisor will *not* be dependent on whether or not they're local.

Instead, they will choose the best advisor to solve their specific issues.

For example, he was answering specific questions that optometrists were dying to get answered and adding value where most financial advisors weren't around topics like whether a leased Lasik machine counted towards the PPP loans.

On his *2020 Vision* podcast (with a rapidly growing audience), he announced he was going to be hosting a webinar for optometrists, specifically how optometrists could use the PPP loans to keep their medical practices running during the difficult pandemic environment.

He had hundreds of prospects on the webinar. And as of March 2021, Adam *still* had prospects on a waiting list to work with him.

And it all came down to leveraging three simple tools to create a compounding effect: His website, his podcast, and a webinar, all narrowly targeted on his target clientele.

> " The more dialed in I became in my focus, the bigger, more frequent, and perfect the opportunities became. It's not if they work with you, it's how they work with you." - *Adam Cmelja*

3. Truth Is...**The riches are in the niches.**

If your ideal audience is currently along the lines of "people approaching retirement" or "people with money" (lol that one's my favorite)...You'll want to go deeper in defining your audience.

For example, it becomes a lot easier to capture attention when you're clearly targeting first-time working moms as opposed to simply working with women.

Not only will you be able to capture more of the RIGHT attention and break through the noisy, constant battle for attention, but you will also:

- ✓ Break through geographic boundaries to be the "go-to" advisor in the country for specific groups of people
- ✓ Have an easier time crafting messages that are impossible for your audience to ignore
- ✓ Know exactly where to find your audience online (and offline!)
- ✓ Lower your rejection rates
- ✓ Become more referable
- ✓ Build a more fulfilling life and practice

I'm not saying you shouldn't continue focusing on people approaching retirement or aim to attract people with a higher net worth.

What I'm saying is: You're doing yourself a major disservice if you don't go deeper than that.

So how do you define your niche or ideal audience?

There are an unfathomable number of ways to dial into your ideal audience.

Before I give you some ideas on things to consider, knowing what *not* to do will make this important decision even easier.

> Don't choose a niche solely based on what, in your perspective, has the greatest financial opportunity.

Is it good if your audience typically has a higher net worth? Sure. Maybe. Depends on the advisor. But it's not everything or always what it seems.

Plus, high net worth (HNW) isn't a niche. It's just not specific enough.

Also, don't put yourself in the same box because you know others have successfully put themselves in that same box.

I'm not saying to avoid niches like doctors, teachers, or federal employees. Those are great examples of groups with specific needs and financial decisions.

But wouldn't you rather create a new lane for yourself? We want to stand out, right?

Dream bigger my friends.

The Self-Minted Millionaire Who Loves to Travel

Let me introduce you to another friend of mine, Derek Notman.

Derek owns a successful RIA who has made millions of dollars 100 percent virtually on a part-time basis. Besides running a practice that has allowed him to build a financial plan on a bullet train in Japan, write an annuity contract at a Starbucks in Ireland, and write life insurance from a beach in South Africa, he's the CEO of a financial advisor course and training company for advisors called Conneqtor.

Derek's target clients are self-minted millionaires who travel the world in luxury. They're not worried about generating wealth. They've already got the money.

His audience is extremely unique. They're smart, savvy, and have created mega-wealth for themselves and their families. They're looking for advisors that speak their language.

For them, their priorities are things like preserving their wealth and protecting their privacy.

Derek also knows that these people value things like destinations for their next luxury vacation, strategies to get more mileage points, how to be a better CEO, etc.

The more specific you are in defining who you want to work with, the easier it is to identify what's important and how you can help.

And it becomes *even easier* when you can also relate to them personally.

As a triple citizen, Delta Million Miler, and a savvy businessman who has been recognized by publications that his ideal audience trusts and respects, Derek can relate to the things that are top of mind to his ideal audience.

"Because I'm interested and passionate about the same things as my ideal clients, creating digital marketing content and funnels is not only easier, but also fun," he said.

Derek has positioned himself—using his content and overall digital presence—as *the* guy for self-minted millionaires who like to travel.

His RIA, Intrepid Wealth Partners, doesn't show up on the first page of an organic Google search results for "Virtual Financial Advisor" on accident. It was by design. And Derek knew the first step was figuring out his niche.

Any advisor can help with retirement planning. *Derek* can help create a luxurious retirement that includes some bucket list travel plans while protecting your wealth.

Why would his clients work with anyone other than him?

There is a limitless number of cohorts that could be yours:

- *Affinities:* Social groups with shared interests and values. Examples: Hobbies, favorite sports teams, personal interests, lifestyle

- *Values:* Groups of people with connections that run deeper than interests and hobbies. These are the things they care the most about, like politics, religion, family
- *Situational:* A situational based niche is based on specific life experiences, events, transitions. Yes, retiring is an example. But so is divorce, selling a business, recently being widowed, having a child, changing careers
- *Industry based:* This may be the most self-explanatory of them all. This would be an audience specific to a job, a position, an industry, or a company. Think about what kind of year 2020 might've been for you if your target audience was in the travel, airline, or hospitality space
- *Demographics-based:* This includes things like culture, gender, age. Generation X differs greatly from the Boomers before them and us Millennials behind them. Men are very different from women. What appeals to people in Texas probably won't resonate with people in NYC. You get the point

In a perfect world, your niche is super specific and a combination of several of the above.

The definition of your ideal audience should be so specific you can plug it into this formula:

"I work with (men/women in this age range) who are (in this stage of life/ facing these decisions) who (see the world and the things that matter the most to them in this way) and want (this outcome for their life)."

When choosing your audience, the world is your oyster.

What is your equivalent of "high school boys hanging around your restaurant to watch the girls on roller skates"?

I know you have clients or prospects who walk in the door and that make you think, "Man. This is not an ideal relationship."

It doesn't have to be that way.

Chapter 4

Make your audience personal to you

I am a firm believer that your audience should be selected NOT based on perceived profitability or what works for the advisor down the street.

Instead, start by what is nearest and dearest to *you*.

For example, Tito Vodka's new campaign, *Vodka for Dog People* stopped me dead in my tracks during a recent trip to Denver.

As a dog person, I can tell you with 100% certainty that if I'm ever buying vodka or ordering a drink and asked what type of vodka I want, I'm choosing Tito's from here on out. Every time.

Obviously, buying vodka isn't the same as choosing an advisor. Plus, I don't drink that much anyways.

But this idea of getting people to stop in their tracks—a.k.a. stop scrolling online—because you are speaking to a shared identity and lifestyle is important.

Chris Smith, the creator of The Campfire Effect™, recently shared a study with me from Fidelity that was absolute gold. We'll hear more from Chris shortly.

Inside this study, Fidelity went deep on identifying what truly matters to affluent investors in their relationships, expectations, and experiences with advisors. Thousands of investors across all demographics were asked, *"Why are you looking for in an advisor?"*

The number one answer was NOT related to their expertise or asset management/planning strategies.

In fact, that was the last item on the list.

The overwhelming response for what they found to be most valuable from a financial advisor fell under one of two categories: *Peace of Mind* and *Fulfillment.*

If you're aiming to create emotional connections and a client base that feels authentic to you, start by looking inside yourself as opposed to the planning services you offer.

When you build a niche around the things you care about and personally relate to, it's much easier to build your business through personal connections.

Who are the people and what are the things that are closest to home?

If you're not sure, start by assessing your current book of clients, closest friends, and family, and looking within yourself.

That's what Adam did.

He found it easy to understand, serve, and want to focus on optometrists because his wife was an optometrist. Boom.

Who are you already attracting? What do your best clients have in common?

If you think you know what direction you want to go in but are unsure of how to tackle it or what to lead with, I encourage you to call your best clients and pick their brain. Your best clients are the best for a reason. They'll likely be super happy to help and appreciate you for showing them you value their opinion.

Once you've defined your ideal audience, the next step is making sure that your messaging is clear and attention grabbing.

Adam does an amazing job at this in his LinkedIn headline with a very simple statement:

"Helping optometrists purposefully plan their personal, professional, and financial life."

Nailed it.

4. Truth Is...**You can't sound like everyone else and expect different results.**

Often, when I ask advisors to pretend I'm a prospect and tell me why I should work with them, the response I get is a list of all the services on their website.

We are an independent firm and team of fiduciaries who do...

- Financial planning
- Retirement planning
- Risk management

- Insurance
- Investment management
- Income planning
- Tax planning
- College planning
- Crypto
- Medicare
- Health insurance
- Long-term care

Okay, got it. Basically, all the services you've listed on your website.

If that's you, I'm really glad you're here.

<u>You may think that's a list of benefits, but it's really just a list of features.</u>

To craft a message about what you do that resonates with potential clients, you have to know, it's not about a product or an investment.

It's a lifestyle. It's a *feeling*.

How to Work with Two Brands—Your Practice and Your Non-Pro it

Let me tell you about an office I know that increased its closing ratio and average client size, both in person and online, by revisiting messaging.

When they first joined Triad Partners, they were already a high performing office that had been in business for 40 plus years. The firm was created and built by the father and had recently been passed to his son. We'll call the son who led the charge on their messaging overhaul, Luke.

Luke's firm initially had two separate brands and forms of messages:

Chapter 4

- *Brand 1:* Luke Advisory Group, which represented a comprehensive planning team for people in or approaching retirement
- *Brand 2:* An "education-based" nonprofit used as entry to venues and audiences to run their retirement seminars

Note, these two brands representing Luke Advisory Group each had their own HQ/office in separate states.

Identifying their messaging initially started off with the goal of:

1. Unifying the two offices/brands
2. Really figuring out how the non-profit fit in

It was a daunting endeavor for this family firm. The legacy in their community over the decades was legendary.

How would a total branding and messaging makeover affect their long-standing reputation and relationships? What if the new messaging resonated in one region, but not another?

And was getting rid of their non-profit really on the table and up for debate?

 A KEY TO SCALE: If you want to achieve scale, your firm should not be named after you. You want to take that trip to Italy, remember?

So, we brought in the big guns and another one of our strategic partners: Chris Smith.

After spending years of success as an advisor, Chris left the client-facing space so he could help other advisors and lean into his passions: language, branding, and leadership. To work with Chris outside of Triad Partners, advisors pay at least $50,000 to get his help uncovering, unlocking, and unleashing their firm's potential and becoming preeminent in their market.

Luke's Advisory Firm, Chris, and our team came together craft an identity and messaging that:

1. Creates success and significance beyond "the business"
2. Is human—and therefore effortless for their team and prospective clients to connect with

"The Side Door" is not the "Main Door"

Let's just get this out of the way. I understand that it's easy to want to come in through the side door.

You ease in; you come across as unassuming, and then BOOM, you ask the prospect to hand over their money.

One example: Marketing yourself primarily as a non-profit and then trying to take prospects down the path of becoming a client once you get them one-on-one.

Here's another: Hosting an event or seminar that is marketed as one about "wills and trusts" to be co-hosted by a local estate planning attorney and then taking a hard pivot with the intention of selling life insurance (with all the tax-free income glory that comes with it).

Let's go to imaginary land and pretend that you're a golfer and you're getting ready to buy some golf clubs before a big upcoming tournament.

You see two advertisements: One from Dick's Sporting Goods with the laundry list of products on its shelves (golf clubs included) and one from the Pro Clubs Boutique.

Who are you going to call?

The Pro Clubs Boutique. All day.

Why? Because they specialize in giving you exactly what you're missing.

Chapter 4

 QUICK REQUEST: Golf not something I can relate to LOL but I have a feeling a majority of you can. Can we find more gender-neutral sports to do in business settings? I want to play. K, thanks.

And how weird would it be if the specialty golf clubs store disguised themselves as an "education-based non-profit for improving your golf swing" who gives you a lesson and then pitches five-figure golf clubs with an assumptive close?

If these tactics have worked for you, great.

But I want you to consider an alternative that will help you speed up your sales process, minimize objections, and become a magnet to people who are ready and excited to work with you.

The Side Door That Should Be the Main Door

Here's the thing about financial services…People DO NOT WORK WITH YOU for your products or your portfolio models or investment returns.

The language that will ultimately attract your ideal clients often has little to do with finances at all.

They want connection.
Purpose.
To make a difference.
Meaning.
To have choices about how they live their lives.
To sleep well at night.
Freedom.
To be *happy*.

The same things that you probably want.

So, filter questions like:
- "What issues does my audience have?"
- "What keeps them up at night?"
- "What issues are they Googling the solutions for?"
- "What do they want?"

Better yet: "What do they need?"

Through the lens of: *"What do they want in their soul as a human being more than anything?"*

Yes, we want to solve financial problems—but I'm challenging you to take your "I help x accomplish y by z" formula to the next level.

> I want your message to hit 'em in-between the eyes and make them think, *"WOW. I've never heard an advisor say that before."*

THAT'S what you'll need to capture people's attention going forward. And not just attention, but the *right* kind of attention.

Luke used a formula that begins with **"We often work with…"**:

"We work with people five years out from retirement or five years post-retirement who don't feel 100 percent confident that they and their family are going to be okay."

This is so simple and profound. That's all people really want in life, including what they want from an advisor, right? To know that they're going to be *okay*.

And then **what you help them do:**

"We help our clients know with certainty that they and their families are going to be okay regardless of what happens so that they can have the courage to truly live their lives."

Sound more like a motivational life coach than an advisor?

Yup. As it should. Because that's really what you are.

Your Heart Benefits Your Audience. Share it.

Your general messaging should also include:

- ✓ What you believe
- ✓ What you stand for
- ✓ Your mission

Why *you*?

Why should they care about *you* as the person delivering the message?

Tell them what you believe and what you stand for. Don't leave it up for interpretation. Don't let them try to guess or come to their own conclusions. Tell them.

When you proactively tell your audience what you're known for and what you stand for, that manifests inside itself.

As Chris said at a Triad event in January 2022, "*Everything you do contributes to either commoditization or preeminence.*"

Your complete story may not be included in every aspect of your digital marketing funnel, but having your messaging mastered will benefit the overall way you attract your ideal audience and set the foundation for the stories you tell in your content.

5. Truth Is...**The only thing that's special about the Big Mac is the packaging.**

Let's revisit The Attention Economy.

This shouldn't come as a shock to you, but not everyone's online content gets the same amount of attention.

The function of "attention" has a couple of parallels to the function of money:

<u>One</u>, it is a bartering tool. Its value is based on what it is being exchanged with. **Every time you pay attention to one thing, you are ignoring, or missing, something else.**

<u>Two</u>, and this one is really interesting—just like there is not an equal distribution of wealth, **there's inequality in how attention is distributed.**

What's Worth Paying Attention To?

There are organizations, situations, and stimuli that receive a LOT of our attention, and others that don't get much at all.

Financial advisors are, unfortunately (lol), not the voices and entities who are capturing a meaningful share of people's attention online.

You're not Kim Kardashian, and nor should you be. But think about who and what you're up against simply by being a financial professional.

The voices inside of the financial services industry who receive the most attention are primarily big companies or personalities with big dollars and resources. We'll refer to those big personalities— think Dave Ramsey—as influencers.

Chapter 4

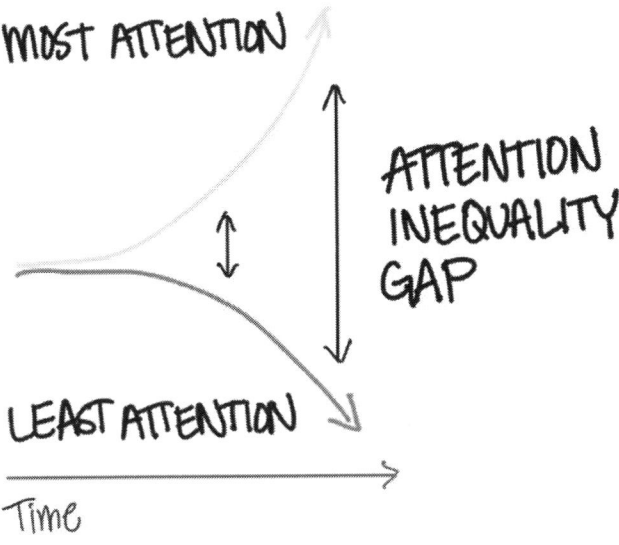

The gap between those who receive the most attention online and those who receive the least—which we'll refer to as **The Attention Inequality Gap**—is widening.

> Create a brand and message that people want to pay attention to ASAP. The Attention Inequality Gap will only get bigger.

The advisors committed to staying ahead of the herd online will prosper, and likely become monopolies for attention in their market.

There's absolutely no reason that can't be you.

So, here's the question: What about the way your firm communicates its value is worth paying attention to?

The answer is *packaging*.

Sell the Whole Package

Today, it's unacceptable to have a long list of things you can do in your back pocket to fire off depending on the problems of who you're talking to.

And remember, people don't care about all the features of the stuff you can do for them.

They just want to know and trust that you can create their ideal outcome and ultimate goal: Being happy.

Think about how the Big Mac—or even burgers in general—are sold. People don't say things like:

- "Come eat our burger because we use six pieces of lettuce and that's the best way to do it."
- "Our tomatoes are perfectly round and have a four-inch diameter every time."
- "Our buns are delicious. If you're not that hungry, we can do a burger with just the buns and leave everything else out in-between. It's the best burger in town."

They aren't selling the ingredients of the burger. They're selling the whole package.

> When your primary method of communicating value is in the weeds, you miss the mark.

Get out of the weeds, bundle everything you do together, and make *the package* the only thing you market.

Doing this inside of your own practice and planning process allows you to:

Chapter 4

- ✓ Stay out of the weeds
- ✓ Streamline your marketing efforts
- ✓ Focus on benefits over features
- ✓ Create something proprietary that your ideal client can't get from anyone else

What's in a Name?

The main difference between a *process* and a **packaged process** is the name.

One office we work with in New England went from a 2 percent close rate to an 80 percent firmwide close rate in 2015 by simply taking their planning process based on the CFP Standard's five focuses of financial planning, giving it a name, and trademarking it.

As of April 2022, there are approximately 92,000 CFP professionals in the United States focusing on income, investments, taxes, legacy, and health care in their planning process.

But there is only one place the mass affluent, a.k.a. those with $500,000+ in investable assets within 5 to 10 years of retirement or recently retired who want to spend their summers in Boston and winters on the beaches down south will go to have their own, personal *Mass Affluent Check Off Your Bucket List and Avoid Cold Winters in Boston Retirement Formula™* [6].

It's hard for that audience to ignore a financial plan that speaks to *their* vision for retirement.

Which do you think has the biggest potential to capture and keep that audience's attention?

---

6. *While the name of the firm and their process has been changed to protect the name of the advisors I'm referencing (and really drive the point home with an ULTRA specific name), the statistics mentioned above are true.*

This list?:

- Financial planning
- Retirement planning
- Risk management
- Insurance
- Investment management
- Income planning
- Tax planning
- College planning
- Crypto
- Medicare
- Health insurance
- Long-term care

Or: *The Mass Affluent Check Off Your Bucket List and Avoid Cold Winters in Boston Retirement Formula™*, brought to New Englanders by a group of independent, comprehensive planners who often work with people who have accumulated a ton of money through hard work and smart planning and want to spend it checking off their bucket list items while having a fiscally reliable escape from the bitter cold winter months at home?

I'm gonna go with the second one.

Chapter 4

Next Steps & Resources You Can Use *Today*

Access the full reports from both Pershing and Fidelity about advisor value propositions and consumer sentiment at: www.truthaboutdm.com/research

Download a guide to help you name and package your process: www.truthaboutdm.com/packaging

Watch a quick video about the biggest issue with advisor branding from a visual perspective—and how to solve it: www.truthaboutdm.com/branding911

Chapter 5

Alignment & Execution

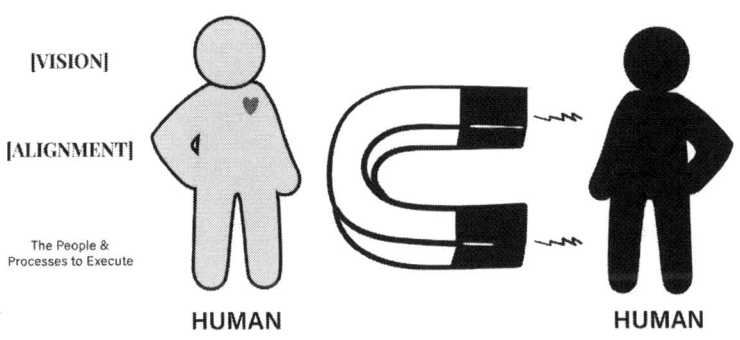

Meet Cameron.

He is the CEO of his firm and, like many other elite advisors I work with or know, he has a passion for marketing. Today, he is a rainmaker, bringing on more assets than he ever thought possible, and has more free time than he's ever had in his career.

But it wasn't always that way.

Let's go back to 2015.

In 2015, Cameron was the type of guy who would get up on stage in front of groups of other advisors and share his ideas about how to bring on $60 million dollars a year in new assets just like him. Other advisors would "ooh" and "ahh" and think to themselves, "WOW. I want to be more like Cameron. I want my firm to have the same success."

What they didn't know was that Cameron was on the verge of burnout. He had fallen out of love with his business. Because the message to advisors is *"more, more, more!"* (do more production, do more marketing, spend more money) the idea of taking his foot off the gas was unfathomable, even though he was spending more nights working and away from the place he really wanted to be: Home. Where he could sit at the dinner table every night, take his sons to hockey practice, etc.

He was extremely successful by industry definitions, and had succeeded by sheer brute force, but was not successful in his personal life or with his health.

Cameron's story has a happy ending that came from him committing to choosing a new and better future.

Cameron's vision dictated that one day he would:

- ✓ Be able to focus on what he loves to do: Marketing and leadership
- ✓ Be surrounded by people who could permanently take everything else off his plate
- ✓ Create predictable processes that made Cameron comfortable spending more time living his life outside of his responsibilities running the firm

In 2020, he and his team brought on a little over $87 million in new assets.

In 2021? His team brought on $178 million dollars in new assets. But Cameron wasn't responsible for all of it. His personal business was only 4 percent of that $178 million—a.k.a. his production was transferred and doused with rocket fuel by his team—and Cameron was finally free to zone in on rain-making activities.

Chapter 5

And here's the best part.

He took 12. Weeks. Off. To spend the summer with his family.

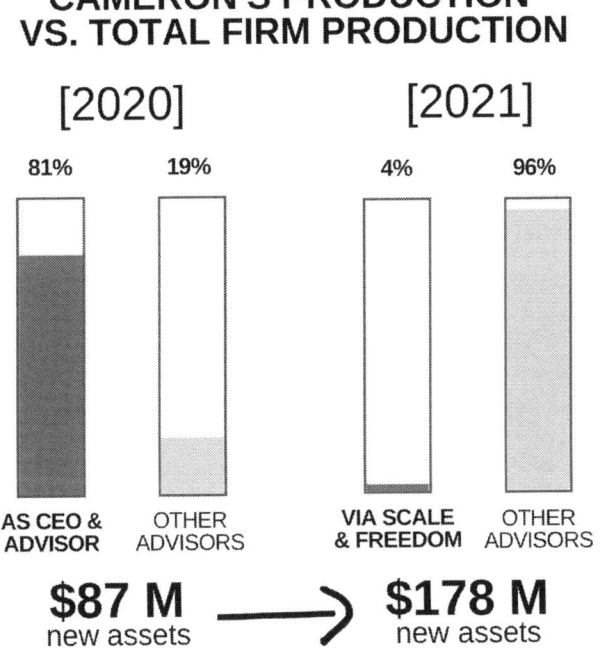

THAT'S the type of story our industry should be telling.

THAT'S the type of outcome our industry should be focused on helping advisors create because in my experience, that's what advisors truly want *more than anything.*

So how did he do it? And what does that have to do with you building an incredible marketing machine (digital or otherwise)?

To put it simply: *Everything.*

Cameron loves digital marketing. This past year, in a single month and with a few hours invested by Cameron, one custom campaign generated over 40 appointments with qualified prospects on his calendar over the course of a month. Guess what kind of campaign it was? A webinar.

Because Cameron's business has leveraged digital marketing inside of his firm's scalable systems, he and his family recently moved to a brand-new part of the country to open a satellite office and start a new chapter for his family and for his business.

That's what it's all about! **Unlimited growth and unlimited freedom.** Boom.

Is that a part of your vision?

There were a lot of small wins that made up Cameron's journey to *true* success—enough for a completely different book—but there are four big ways Cameron's vision allowed him to lay the foundation for better marketing through internal alignment and execution.

 QUICK SIDE NOTE: I know that some of you picture a team with 30 (or more) people on staff to bring on $178 million in new assets in a year. But check it out. They did it with 17 people.

This chapter is about how to scale—which doesn't necessarily mean building a massive enterprise. As far as we're concerned...

> Achieving scale means creating more freedom in your business AND life.

In this chapter you'll learn how you can align your team, execute on that alignment, and how that will inform how you tackle digital marketing—just like Cameron.

Chapter 5

1. Truth Is...**McDonald's secret sauce is not something you can find on the menu.**

Going back to the McDonalds' success story for a second, let's look at two things that allowed them to have the success they had: Systemization and scale.

Who's working the registers and who's making the Big Macs?

The Big Mac wasn't invented until the eighties. McDonald's double-decker hamburger isn't the thing that turned the opportunity to open a franchise into a national phenomenon. McDonald's did a lot of things right for decades before the introduction of the Big Mac.

But it all began, and was made possible by, the *Speedee Service System* introduced in 1948. People just could not believe how fast their meals were served.

Bonus points for McDonald's and that speed because regardless of whatever the heck is in those burger patties today, they were 100 percent high-quality, freshly ground beef patties.

The thing that made their process "Speedee" was the *systems* and the efficiencies those systems created.

The assembly line, invented by Henry Ford in 1913, was still a very new technology that had transformed the way automobiles were created.

And Mack and Richard McDonald took a page from Ford's playbook to create their own version of an assembly line.

The goal was to lower prices/cost of doing business and increase the number of people they served—a.k.a. quantity of sales—and overall speed.

Prior to Ford's assembly line, each worker was responsible for building the whole vehicle from start to finish. The assembly line innovation created specialization and efficiency for the automobile manufacturer because each person was expertly responsible for only doing one or two things for any given vehicle.

That's what McDonald's did.

Every single member of its 12-man staff had one job and one job only. Whether it was grilling the patties, adding the condiments, making the french fries, or running the cash register… McDonald's mechanized its operation by specializing, dividing, and conquering.

This was a HUGE DEAL. For example, they were able to cook 20 more burgers an hour by simply moving the ketchup dispenser *three inches*.

Remember when we talked about how McDonald's whittled its menu down to nine items?

Aside from being the most popular options on the menu, they were all handheld. In other words, McDonald's became more efficient by eliminating all silverware, glassware, etc. (and all the washing, drying, storing labor that went with it).

Going forward, all McDonald's needed was paper wraps and disposable cups. Boom.

They were the fastest, cheapest, and best burger spot in town. The McDonalds brothers were having more fun at work than ever before and even created a mascot named *Speedee*. It was their thing.

Chapter 5

Do me a favor and imagine for a second that you're at a McDonald's cash register. You just ordered yourself a Big Mac. If your stomach hurts just thinking about it, same. But bear with me—this is important.

What happens when you give your order to the person at the register?

Pointing out what *doesn't* happen is a bit more illuminating than what does.

The person who takes your order doesn't say, "Cool, thanks for the order, we're on it!" and then dash to the back to fry (probably microwave) the burger.

They're not washing their hands and heating up the griddle.

They submit a ticket that goes back to the kitchen directly to, and with specific directions for, the person who makes the Big Macs. You take a number, step aside, and the cashier takes the order of the next person in line.

McDonald's gets busy? They open another cash register. The cashier follows the exact same protocols.

In recent years, the self-service model got even faster when McDonald's implemented a new service window for customers who had already been served. No more bottleneck at the cash register for coke refills.

Today, you don't even need to say the name of what you're ordering. You just tell them the number.

McDonald's dialed in service was incredibly easy to duplicate. Every little thing—even down to the number of pickles on every burger—was part of an established process.

In 2022, there are more than 37,000 places in 120 different countries where you can go to a McDonald's.

It was a weird eye-sore, but when Joe and I took a trip to Thailand in 2018, there were McDonald's all over the place!

Even on the other side of the world, we were within couple miles of being able to buy a Big Mac (or a Mc-Whatever) at any given moment.

What can we take from this and apply to our firm and digital marketing?

More than we have time for here. So, we'll simplify it. Don't worry about opening an office in the South Pacific. Just think about your day-to-day business and consider this:

Inside your practice, if you're the advisor, you're the one at the cash register. You meet with potential customers. But in this position as the "cashier", many advisors don't stick to "the register" to keep serving new paying customers.

After the advisor takes the order—a.k.a. meets with a prospect—they're putting on a hair net and dashing back to the kitchen to make the Big Mac—a.k.a. build the plan.

BUT! They're not *only* doing the planning. Many are also doing the service work, managing assets, and running the business. And now you're supposed to add digital marketing to your plate?

Does that sound like you? How can anyone be expected to do it all, in the way that most advisors currently operate, and do it well?

If you are doing it all, and you're doing it well, that's great. But how are you holding up, friend?

Wouldn't you rather have the freedom to specialize in only the things that you love to do? The highest and best use of your time? Creating the vision, bringing on new clients, and pushing the business forward?

If you want to grow and maximize your efforts across the board—not just digitally—**creating your own duplicatable systems is foundational.**

Otherwise, you will spend your time spinning your wheels, wasting a lot of time and money, missing quality time with your loved ones, and losing the war for attention online (and potentially in person too).

2. Truth Is...**You can't boil the ocean.**

Of all the business development frameworks we coach to at Triad Partners, there is one model that resonates the MOST with top-performing advisors: The Four Phases to Scale.

For now, we'll just focus on making the shift from Phase One to Phase Two—a game-changing transformation that 90 percent of advisors never experience.

We start with the understanding that your financial advisory business is not just ONE business. It's three.

When you first start out in the business, you're usually a one-man (or one-woman) show. This is what we refer to as The Advisor in Charge Model.

You're grinding, moving and shaking, slowly gaining confidence.

As you begin to see success, you think to yourself, *"It's working!"*

Eventually, one day, you realize, "Wow! I could use some help." So, you hire an assistant and begin delegating some of the low value tasks.

Chapter 5

Good move because it frees up some of your time to focus on growing the business.

The success continues, and soon enough, you're ready to hire again.

So, you bring on another assistant. And the cycle continues.

 TRUE STORY: One advisor I know surrounded himself by eight of these assistants or helpers. Sure, he was "successful" by industry definition—he was bringing in $40 million dollars a year in new assets. One of those guys recognized on stages and collecting trophies for production. But he inevitably burned out and ultimately sold his "successful" practice for pennies on the dollar.

While this model helps free up time by surrounding you with people who can help you check boxes off your to-do list, there are two issues here:

Issue #1:

The advisor is still responsible for all the thinking and activities that drive growth for their business. You can delegate *tasks* like office management, handling the calendar, and answering the phone. But the high-value stuff and all the *thinking* comes back to the advisor. This includes the vision, marketing, revenue, relationships, etc.

Yes, we are creating *some* freedom, but the business is still completely dependent on you to run, a.k.a. you're not scheduling that trip to Italy anytime soon without worrying that your business will completely be put on hold.

<u>Issue #2:</u>

These "assistants" are typically generalists, not specialists. You usually see these individuals compensated in the $15 to $25/hour range. Of course, there are outliers. But mostly, advisors end up surrounding themselves with order takers who are not empowered or do not have the skillset to help take high value tasks off the advisor's plate.

Eventually, if you want to break free from The Advisor in Charge Model and operate more like a business owner, you start by doing two things:

1. **Segmenting your business into three different parts: Marketing, Sales, and Operations**

[SEGMENTING YOUR BUSINESS]

2. **Hiring SPECIALISTS and A-PLAYERS inside those three areas and ultimately get some of the thinking and responsibilities off your desk**

Chapter 5

I often hear advisors say, "Well, I mean I have an assistant, but she's definitely not an order taker…She does a great job helping me with marketing, she helps prepare for meetings and with my compliance too…"

Sounds like she's super helpful and doing a great job. Truly.

But she is not operating as a specialist.

You cannot maximize your firm's output and your freedom to live your life (AND build a killer digital marketing system) without *specialists*.

And long-term, you cannot completely rely on working with strictly third-party specialists.

Why? Because:

> You can't outsource your core competencies.

I'd argue that one of your *core* competencies is how you build trust and relationships. Your authentic and magnetic value proposition. Your approach to solving problems, adding value, and changing lives. The client experience. Do you really want a third-party dictating and defining what that means?

Once you've established your three segments, a.k.a. laid the foundation for your org chart, begin looking at your current staff and potential hiring opportunities by looking for people who can take over those tasks and workflows.

This is not just about simply delegating. It's about having specialized teammates who can be empowered to own their area of expertise.

For marketing, that means either empowering someone on your team, or hiring a specialist to run/manage your marketing efforts. This can include:

- Ideation for new campaigns
- Creative thinking
- Communication
- Social media
- Content management systems
- Analytics and attention to detail
- Mobile user experience and advertising
- Video content
- Layout and design
- Cross campaign coordination
- Evaluating and editing content or campaigns
- Proficiency in copywriting
- Vendor management
- Event management
- Campaign management
- Vendor management

Chapter 5

I would say that's one less thing on your plate so that you can focus on meeting with clients and prospects...But hiring a true marketing specialist to assist you in your endeavor to have a fantastic marketing team, digital or not, is more like taking 15 things off your plate.

Remember that office in New England who transformed their business by packaging their process? They brought on $257 million in new assets in 2021...And one of their key philosophies is this:

Instead of waiting to hire until you realize your team doesn't have the bandwidth to handle the growth, pre-hire in *anticipation* of growth based on your 3 to 5 year plan to achieve your vision.

Playing catch-up inside your org chart is a slippery slope.

You, my friend, are putting in amazing work to get people in the door. You don't need to fly by the seat of your pants every time you bring a marketing campaign to life.

You don't need to fly by the seat of your pants at all.

Hiring the right kind of help is essential to getting off the hamster wheel.

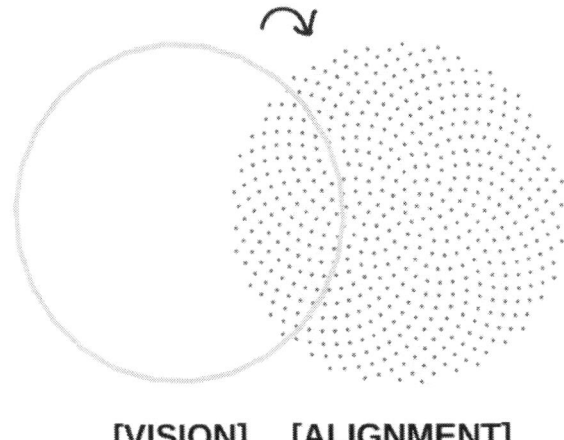

[VISION]   [ALIGNMENT]

Let Experts Do Expert Things

I'm not saying everything should be brought in-house or built by someone on your internal staff. Some things are *100 percent* worth outsourcing. But maybe not the way our industry has gotten used to.

One of the mottos in our office is: "Let experts do expert things."

I think it serves us to examine what it means to be an expert.

An expert is somebody who has a comprehensive and authoritative knowledge base, deep competence, skill, and experience through practice and education.

> When you're looking for experts who can help grow your business, look for the best experts PERIOD.

Not *just* the best in our industry.

Those experts should be aligned with and share your vision and goals. They should be excited to apply their expertise to your specific vision as opposed to their own vision, efficiencies, and templates.

Should we avoid experts inside our industry? Nope. Not at all. The learning curve related to compliance and the advisor value proposition when you bring in an outside-industry expert is very real.

There are some incredible minds inside our industry who will create and deliver custom, innovative solutions.

Just, don't forget, there are a *ton* of experts outside of, and way ahead of, many industry experts. Think big.

The best advisors in the country have done the same.

Chapter 5

The Difference When You Work With a Digital Marketing Expert

One day, Cameron reached out in a panic. His mailers had bombed, registrations were almost non-existent, and his dinner event was rapidly approaching.

He asked, "Is there anything you guys can do to help?"

We brought in some world-renowned marketing experts—we'll call the brains behind the operation "Tom". Remember that name. We'll come back to him later to dig deeper into how marketing experts who work with A-List celebrities and global business thought leaders approach digital.

Tom's team is typically hired to build funnels that fill stadiums for big-ticket events and speakers.

When we approached him to see if he could help fill a room with 30 people for an hour of education and a free steak, he laughed. He was definitely down to help. So, we got to work.

In the first 24 hours of Cameron's ad campaign launching, we were able to fill up his seminars in two days with:

- ✓ 34 households
- ✓ $405 in total ad spend (that's $11/registrant!)
- ✓ Had a show up rate of 76 percent of all that registered

Let that sink in. These results are astonishing.

The average show-up rate, meaning the number of people who attend after registering, for an educational event marketed by a standard industry campaign is usually around 40 percent.

The show-up rate for Cameron's event, which was marketed by experts who were laser-focused on his unique value proposition, was a whopping *76 percent.*

In fact, we so severely underestimated how many people would show up that there was a line out the restaurant's door for people who hadn't even registered but simply heard about the event and wanted to be there.

...And for *less than $500* in ad spend.

Insane!

Should we be surprised? Probably not.

Experts do expert things.

Go find the right internal and external specialists to bring your unique vision to life.

 WANT TO SEE CAMERON'S EVENT FUNNEL?: You can check out a full map of his actual funnel at: www.truthaboutdm.com/eventfunnel

3. Truth Is...**You need to know your numbers.**

I once worked with an advisor who tracked nothing besides revenue.

He was always very confident about where things were going because no matter what was going on with his marketing, his team, the weather... Revenue was always positive.

Until one day, it wasn't.

You can generate revenue from inside your book of business all day long. Replacements, picking up new assets, clients turning 59 1/2...

But you can't do it forever. You have to keep bringing on new clients and setting brand-new first appointments.

The number of first appointments you book is the leading indicator of firm growth—NOT revenue.

If you are a growth-focused firm, you gotta have a laser focus on strategies that fill your calendar with firsts.

By the time this advisor realized this, he was basically back at square one for marketing.

Don't make the same mistake and remember this:

> Just because your revenue is up doesn't mean you're *growing*.

Imagine you're in Vegas and you've got 10 different slot machines to pick from. If you knew which machines would consistently give you back more winnings than what you gambled, you would probably sit at those slot machines all day long.

Each of your marketing funnels is a slot machine.

The only way to know that any funnel is a winning slot machine and avoid gambling away your hard-earned marketing dollars is by *knowing your numbers*.

Knowing your numbers means having systems (and a teammate who owns those systems) who will leverage your CRM, marketing tools, and other resources available to track:

- ✓ Source of prospect (because I know you're doing more than just digital)
- ✓ Number of leads per campaign
- ✓ Number of clients per campaign
- ✓ How many of those leads booked appointments
- ✓ How many of those leads showed up for the appointments
- ✓ How many of those leads turned into clients
- ✓ Avg. net worth
- ✓ Avg. revenue for new client gained (short-term and long-term)
- ✓ Cost per lead
- ✓ Cost per appointment
- ✓ Cost per client
- ✓ How long it took for the lead to become a client

You cannot—and I mean CANNOT—make intelligent decisions about your marketing efforts until you know your numbers.

Otherwise, you will fall into the trap that I have seen time and time again (and I have even fallen victim to). Making counterproductive, uninformed, emotional decisions.

Math Over Emotions

I'll give you two common examples here—and we'll start with seminars.

Advisors often say that they hate doing dinner seminars and that they don't work. When we drill down on where these feelings are coming from, they're never related to the results.

I hear things like, "They're too expensive," or "There are too many plate lickers."

These statements are usually accompanied by an underlying frustration about the evenings spent away from their families.

But then we do the math, and we find that the ROI is 6:1.

Expensive, maybe.

Plate lickers, for sure.

But ineffective? I don't think so.

Here's another way this shows up. Advisors will heavily invest in a specific funnel or activity simply because it makes them *feel* good.

Good example: Radio.

People love the idea of being on the radio and having their own show. Advisors see other advisors crushing it on radio and want to do the same. It certainly creates credibility, which is a hard thing to quantitatively measure, but is always a plus. And, although most high-performing advisors we work with have shifted away from radio, it has historically been a rainmaker.

Truth is, even when radio was at its *peak*, the numbers weren't the same for everyone. The numbers are never the same for EVERYONE, regardless of what the marketing activity is. Using the example of radio, the cost of airtime in Chicago, Illinois is very different in Lexington, Kentucky. The number of listeners varies. Not everyone gets the same results.

Is there value in having a radio show? Sure. But how do the numbers look? Are you investing in your business or flushing money down the toilet on something that makes you feel good?

Math over emotions all day long.

4. Truth Is...**Systems are the key to execution.**

The key to scaling your business is making creating duplicatable systems everywhere you can. The more you can document and systematize your current efforts, the more efficient your team will be and the less will bottleneck on you.

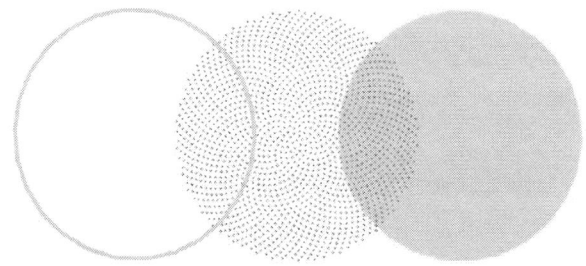

VISION.   ALIGNMENT.   EXECUTION.

Here's how this looks for way too many advisors:

- Hear great idea
- Say, "Let's do it!"
- Tell their team they're doing it
- Fly by the seat of their pants
- Reactively prepare (vs. proactively execute based on predetermined protocols)
- Do their best (but unintentionally half-ass it)
- See how they feel (hopefully they feel good, but everyone is probably exhausted and maybe a little stressed out)
- Either do it again or never do it again
- But probably do it again

I know this might make you cringe just thinking about it, but if you're also nodding your head because you can relate, you probably have some gaps in your internal operations.

Again, unless you are an advisor who wants and has the freedom to solely focus on marketing, marketing should not be falling entirely on your lap.

You have to leverage a team.

But! Leveraging a team doesn't mean transferring the chaos. They will not be able to do their best work if they're constantly suffering from whiplash every time there's a new shiny object to chase.

We already know that hiring a specialist to spearhead your firm's initiatives is fundamental to creating killer outcomes. So, the question becomes: When you hire that specialist, how do you relinquish control without completely giving up control?

There are several ways to delegate depending on the project and the people involved.

For simplicity's sake, we'll lean on one that has proven effective for advisors at any stage on their journey to scale and refer back to it throughout the book.

Allow me to introduce The 10-80-10 Rule, made famous by global business thought leader John Maxwell.

This means being involved in the first 10 percent and the last 10 percent.

Let's say you want to post more videos. We already know that people connect with people, and you'll need to be involved.

Step one is the first 10 percent.

You define your vision, the objectives, and what an ideal outcome looks like. Share this vision with the specialist, or team of specialists, who oversee your video content and marketing and make sure everyone is *crystal clear* on the goal of the campaign.

Empower your team with the vision and guidelines to run with it and set 'em loose.

And that's step two, or where 80 percent of the execution happens.

Your marketing team—in-house or outsourced— optimizes the video script, helps schedule a time and setting for the video to be recorded, edits of the video, repurposes the video for other types of content (which we'll talk more about later), and makes sure the back end of the campaign is set up (which includes, but is not limited to, writing the emails, builds the landing page, etc).

Are they ready to execute? Nope. Not yet. Because step three means bringing it back to you.

Step three is the final 10 percent where you approve and/or tweak to ensure it'll resonate with your ideal client and represent your voice and value.

Besides the obvious benefit, which is freeing up your time, there is another massive benefit: You are empowering your team to feel like they have ownership of the task and will feel pride when the campaign comes to life.

Just like attention can be compared to money as a form of currency to be exchanged, so is time.

Every time you say *"yes!"* to a task or activity, you're saying *"no"* to something else.

Part of being a good CEO is knowing where your time is best spent.

It is not in the weeds of where you are not the expert. Nor is it being completely hands off. You must proactively empower your team of specialists to do what they do best.

According to a 2020 survey completed by Kitces and his research team titled *The Importance of Client Acquisition Costs and the J-Curve of Lifetime Client Value*, the biggest expense to bring on a new client is time.

It's not the money you spend on labor, vendors, marketing assets, technology, and testing new opportunities. The monetary expenses are, on average, a mere 17 percent.

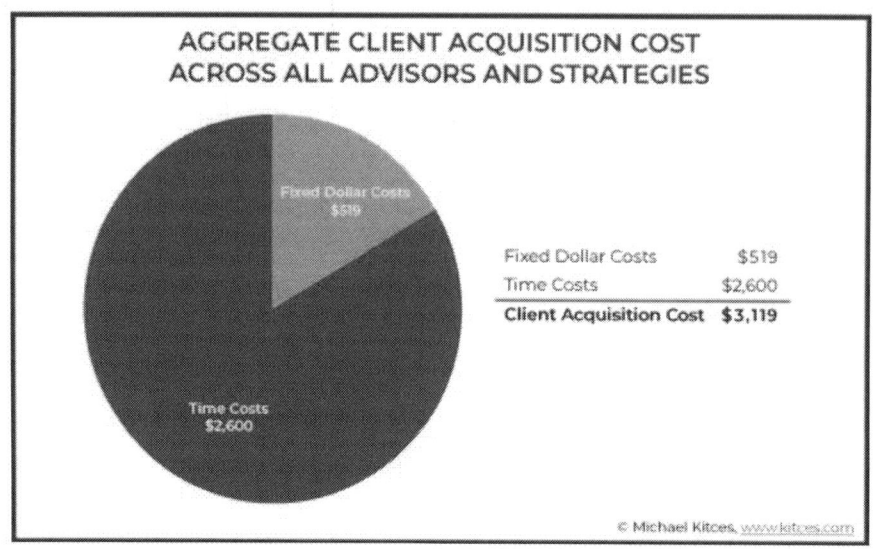

As for the rest? According to the data—across all advisors and strategies to acquire a new client—**83 percent of the costs come down to time.**

Yes, we know that we need to show up in our marketing.

We know that we cannot outsource our core competencies.

But are you involved in every single meeting and discussion about the project? Doing all the research? The first line of defense for every marketing company pitching a new campaign?

Your digital marketing outcomes, as well as the efforts that create them, need to be supported by a business with an infrastructure that will support it.

These processes and transferring ownership to a teammate should include things like:

- Who does what (and when)
- The criteria for success

- What tools are used
- Deadlines
- Checklists for your workflows
- Templates and technology to streamline tasks

And guess what? The more successful you become, the more you'll have to keep building out that org chart.

Once you have all your systems in place, it gets 100 times easier to get new hires up to speed, actively contributing, operating with clarity, and in a position to be the best teammate they can be.

And speaking of new hires…If you want to bring on talent, especially *specialized* talent, you have to know what job applicants are looking for.

The next generation for our industry—a.k.a. millennials like me—want to work for companies that have an inspiring vision and a strong brand. They will choose the organization with the greatest upside potential and opportunities to grow. And they'll be looking for the systems, processes, and paths from employers to back it up.

Your lack of work-life balance will not be enticing to a potential new hire.

Especially today. Work-life balance has never been more important.

If the business isn't set up properly *and* you aren't making an effort to leverage technology and lean into digital marketing, you're not going to attract the level of talent you'll need to take your business (and life) to the next level.

As I mentioned earlier, there are many other things that contributed to Cameron's massive evolution from burnout to bliss. And I'll continue sharing actionable insights for you as the leader on your team throughout this book.

But, if there's nothing else you take from this chapter, know this: **Business is a team sport, and the best teams have a solid playbook.**

Next Steps & Resources You Can Use *Today*

If Cameron's story resonates with you and you are a high-performing and comprehensive financial advisor bringing on more than $10 million a year in FIA's, let's have a conversation: www.truthaboutdm.com/convo

Grab a sample spreadsheet you can use to understand your marketing numbers and make informed decisions about your marketing at: www.truthaboutdm.com/mathoveremotions

If you'd like a framework that can help you leverage The 10-80-10 Rule next time you go to delegate or outsource marketing support, access it here: www.truthaboutdm.com/108010

To read Kitces' full study, *The Most Efficient Financial Advisor Marketing Strategies And The True Cost To Acquire A Client*, head to: www.truthaboutdm.com/kitcesresearch

PART TWO:

Creating
Success Online & Unlocking Unlimited Growth Potential Using
The Magnetic Digital Advisor Model™

Chapter 6

Materializing Your Online Relationships

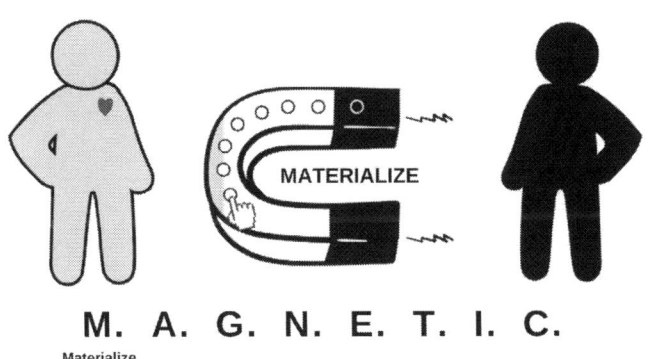

As we know, at the end of every transaction is a human. Even when it's an online, self-managed account, there is always a human. Luckily for you, there's a human on your end as well.

The biggest misconception about digital marketing is that it's completely automated. The funnel runs and appointments show up on your calendar with no effort from a human.

I hear it all the time:

"I post on social media, but I haven't gained any clients."

"I have an automated webinar, but I rarely get any appointments."

"I've never picked up a client from the emails that go to my database."

In each of these scenarios, and the dozens of other common complaints I hear about "why digital doesn't work," I find there's always one major factor in common: There isn't a human touch on the advisor's end to engage the audience and take the conversation offline.

There are four major things that you can (and should) consider implementing if you are also looking to bring on more ideal clients, speed up your sales process, and materialize all of the leads you've generated with your digital marketing:

1. Creating human touches
2. Hiring a dedicated appointment setter. And they can't just be *anyone* who knows how to use a phone
3. Complementing your digital marketing with other non-digital, but highly personal strategies such as handwritten notes, packages, etc.
4. Establishing trust and a great virtual first impression

1. Truth Is...**There's got to be a human on the other side of the line.**

Michael is one of the most successful advisors I know. He started off in the business as a receptionist at a planning firm and over the course of his career, he has worn every single hat in the business. Today, he is in his early thirties, and after a few short years of starting fresh and building his own firm, he is the CEO of a team bringing on north of $60 million in assets a year.

When 2020 hit, he was one of the first to proactively go all in on digital. But the results weren't there.

For 18 months, he poured cash into webinars, rebuilding his website, and creating a presence online. He leaned further into TV and radio when his live educational events came off the table. This superstar had very little to show for his efforts aside from a thick stack of invoices.

He called our team searching for answers.

"I thought digital was the future!?"

The solution was a lot less about digital marketing and more about his firm's infrastructure.

As deep as Michael's org chart was, he was missing one key person.

Not a new email sequence, not a new lead magnet, not a different webinar topic.

Even as a firm with a highly specialized org chart with a ton of depth in the marketing department, he was missing the most important teammate of all: **An appointment setter.**

Someone whose sole job is to reach out to everyone who engages with his marketing efforts. A human.

Within *three months* of hiring an appointment setter, she had paid for herself.

Not only did Michael's conversion rate go up by over *800 percent,* but he also observed an additional (and very unexpected) improvement for his firm: He was closing higher net-worth clients in half the time.

Why?

Because there was a real person serving as his team's hype woman. Not a robot. Not an advisor who was trying to sell them something.

A human.

Onboard a Phone Warrior

I know that there are advisors who call and follow up with leads. If that's you, bravo. Working the phone is not for the faint of heart.

But consider this:

If you're the Lead Advisor and/or CEO and/or Founder, but you're also the person calling them, trying to chase them down…The perception of your value immediately decreases.

Don't you have something better to do? (Yes.)

As a hype person, the person making outbound calls and setting appointments is talking about how awesome you are and how busy you are. They'll look for and confirm opportunities to serve them, while protecting everyone's time—yours included. If it makes sense, they'll get them excited about the potential alignment and be the hook up to get the prospect on the calendar.

In this scenario, you're busy, but you're an outstanding firm who is willing to take the time to see if you can help them. Getting on your calendar feels like a win.

This is a *completely* different dynamic than having the advisor make the dials.

Hiring a phone warrior resulted in Michael bringing on his biggest client to-date.

Now, hiring the appointment setter was just the tip of the iceberg.

2. Truth Is...**You need humans at the bottom of your funnel. And those humans better be hungry.**

Earlier, I mentioned that Michael's phone warrior brought on his firm's biggest client, representing $12.7 million in new assets to their book.

What did the appointment setter do to get that client on the calendar?

He called him eight times over a two-week period.

When was the last time you called a prospect eight times in a two-week period? Or even within a month? Would you even want to if you could?

> A good appointment setter is worth their weight in gold.

They shouldn't be a standalone outside party. They need to be integrated with the rest of your team, have a unique skill set, and be compensated/incentivized appropriately.

Go Find Your Appointment-Setting Unicorn

I repeat, a good appointment setter is worth their weight in gold.

It's your appointment setter's job to get appointments on the calendar by any means necessary.

In other words, you need them to be fearless, meaning they are:

- Unafraid to pick up the phone and call strangers
- Unafraid of rejection, objections, or negativity from the person on the other side of the phone

- Undaunted by the pressure of being the liaison that puts them on your calendar
- Unphased by the demands of the position

This is an *important job*.

Another office I work with, bringing on $30 million a year in new money, made an appointment setter their first hire.

First! Hire!

That's how important this is. But, finding the right appointment setter isn't easy.

Aside from being fearless, they must understand you and your business enough to be consistent with your message. They need to be easy to talk to and great with people. You'll want them to be organized, proactive, and detail oriented.

Truth be told, they are unicorns.

But they're out there. So go find your unicorn and pay them well.

There is not a single position with a higher ROI than your appointment setter.

 DON'T FORGET: In a virtual world, every single person in your office who interacts with potential prospects over the phone must be reminded and held accountable for how they come across over the phone. Not just your appointment setter. How does the way your team sounds on the phone contribute to or detract from your credibility?

3. Truth Is...**Turning online prospects into real life clients requires personalization.**

Making outbound calls is not the only way to get appointments with people who are toward the bottom of the funnel.

In conjunction with having a phone warrior focused on building relationships with your prospects, implement other highly personalized human touches.

Embracing all the things that make you human by including *personal touches* in all of your interactions will make a difference in bringing people over that finish line.

Here's how to do it.

Gifting

For one of the mastermind calls inside the Triad Partners Community, we brought in John Ruhlin. John is an international best-selling author of the book *Giftology*, the CEO of the Ruhlin Group, a company that serves Fortune 100 companies by creating exceptional client experiences via gifting, and a world-renowned speaker and thought leader.

He shared a metaphor that will change the way you will think about how you use gifts in your business forever.

Imagine if one of your wedding guests left a gift in a box that was branded with the logo of the company you work at. You'd be like, "What?"

You would never do that in a personal setting. So why do we do it in business?

The gifts you give to prospects (as well as clients) are delivery vehicles and representations of an emotional connection. **Gifts are symbols of the value you place on the relationship.**

Here is what a gift *is not*:
Your company swag.

Remember, it's not B2B or B2C, it's H2H. It's all about relationships. The gifts you give should not be the equivalent of giving the recipient a chance to be a walking billboard.

John said, *"When all you do is give 'swag', you're telling the receiver that 'this is a business relationship' more than a personal relationship."*

A gift, on the other hand, is a representation of how much you value the relationship on a human level. A thoughtful, personalized gift creates intimacy and makes the recipient feel seen.

Don't throw out your swag. There is a time and place for it.

But when you're engaging with people via *gifts* and aiming to materialize the relationship, think about putting their name on the gift instead of your own. Something that means more to *them* than it does to you.

Handwritten Notes:

Always, always include a handwritten note.

When you don't have enough personal information to send a super personalized gift, there are a thousand opportunities to send a handwritten note. These situations are similar to situations in which you'd send a video message, so we'll talk about them in a second.

Identify someone who can write your handwritten notes and find someone who can craft the messages. There are some *great* tools that allow you to automate and systematize your handwritten notes out there.

Chapter 6

Video Emails:

Video emails are the bomb. They allow you to add more of a human element to your message so you can say, *"Hey! This message is for YOU!"* We'll talk more later about how to leverage video, but when you're on the one-yard line, personalized video emails are powerful.

Use video emails:

- ✓ Before an event or meeting to introduce yourself, thank attendees for their time, and let them know whatever they need to know
- ✓ To provide visual instructions on how to park and where to go for the seminar
- ✓ After attending a webinar, seminar, or first meeting, send a recap about what was discussed and next steps
- ✓ To nurture leads by highlighting case studies or educational content in video form
- ✓ To explain complex topics or soften the blow when things don't go as planned
- ✓ For birthdays, milestones, anniversaries

All great reasons to send handwritten notes, by the way.

Here's a quick hack. If you're going to take the time to record a personal video for a prospect, make sure they know it's for *them.*

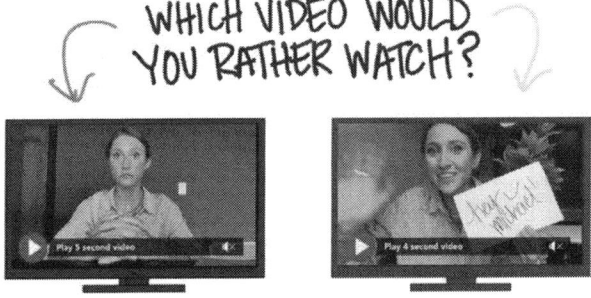

This can be done, for example, by purchasing a whiteboard and writing a message on it that shows the message is for them, and acts as a headline for why they should watch the video.

For example, one time, there was an individual I wasn't having much luck re-connecting with. We'll call him Billy. We had a great first conversation, had a second meeting scheduled, got the message about needing to raincheck (for a very valid reason), and three months later, I hadn't been able to get back in touch.

But we had one thing in common. And that was one of the major drivers for me wanting to reconnect with him. He's a MAJOR dog lover and does a really cool video series with his pup, who we'll call Lola. (RIP to the dog that raised me, Lola.)

So, I recorded a video email, just like the example above, and wrote *"HEY BILLY! Tell LOLA I'm SO SORRY!"*

How could he NOT watch that video?

Don't worry, I did not harm his dog.

But the message basically said, *"Hey Billy, hope you got my package, I'm kicking myself for not including some of the dog treats I get locally that MY dog is obsessed with, so tell Lola I'm sorry I left her out of the delivery. And by the way, x, y, z offer."*

Guess who answered after three months of radio silence, wanting to book a call for the following week? Billy.

Sometimes you don't know enough about them yet to get *that* personal, but even simply adding a "thank you!" or asking a question on the whiteboard with their name on it will make a difference.

For example, let's say one of your prospects just turned 62. You might write on the whiteboard for your video email *"Hey John! How does it feel!?"*

John, your hypothetical prospect, will think, *"Wait. How does what feel?"* and won't be able to resist playing your video.

Boom. The door is open for a video about Social Security claiming strategies and a message that could begin like, *"Hey John! Happy Birthday and CONGRATS! How does it feel being 62 and officially eligible to file for Social Security?"*

When you are asked a question, even if it's as passive as a sign on a random billboard, your mind subconsciously wants to answer it.

Leading with questions in your emails, videos, etc., gives you a chance to create a dialogue.

I'm going to take a hard stance that video is not clickbait when it comes from the heart and you're adding value.

One last comment here: The video will feel a lot more personal if you look at the camera instead of yourself when you record. It emulates eye contact. If it helps, put a photo of someone you love right next to the camera. Your messages will immediately feel more natural and intimate.

Interact…With Everyone

One way to get more personal is to start adding and following people on social media. That's how you pick up on small, personal opportunities of impact, like the one with Billy and Lola.

When you have a prospect who's *thiiiiiis close* to converting who you haven't been able to connect with, get out there and start engaging with their social media content.

When you do so consistently, prospects will eventually engage back.

Anyone who likes or comments on a piece of content is raising their hand, regardless of where they are in your funnel. **Every like and every comment is an *opportunity*!**

Do. Not. Ignore. Likes. And Comments.

Think about it this way:

Imagine you're having a conversation with some people you don't know very well. If you tell a joke or a story, and someone in this group of people laughs at the joke or adds their two cents, will you ignore them?

Probably not. Especially if it's someone you don't know that well.

In real life you'd lean into this connection point and look for ways to build on it because you're interested in the same things. You might even exchange phone numbers to stay in touch.

On social media, it works the same way. You could (and should) respond to comments on your posts. But I want you to take it a step further and move the conversation into a more intimate setting by sending them a conversational direct message.

Conversational message does not mean a (directly or indirectly) salesy message. You're just building on the connection with the goal of adding value and engaging further.

<u>*Examples*</u>:

- "Hey, I saw you liked my post. Thanks so much for showing it some love!! Curious—what's your experience with (your post)?"
- "Hi! That was a great point you made. So interesting for x, y, z reasons. Tell me more about your experience."
- "That was such a good question on my post. I've heard that question a bunch. Here's what I've seen, in my experience. Is that helpful? What's your experience?"

Chapter 6

 EASY PSYCHOLOGY HACK: You're much more likely to get questions answered when you tell them why you're asking.

This is so much more effective than sending someone a random message telling them to use your scheduling link to set up a time to discuss rolling over their 401k. Like, you don't even know if they have a 401k!

Moving the conversation from the timeline to their inbox is also a great gauge of where they are in their relationship with you (and your value proposition if the content is more related to your value proposition).

Will these conversations immediately translate into offline phone conversations? No.

And that's okay! Because now you know.

If they will not respond to a compliment, your gratitude, a prompt to talk about themselves or something they're interested in, it's highly unlikely they want to hop on a call or commit to a full-blown meeting.

And if nothing else, you're building trust and rapport, breaking the seal on a one-to-one conversation, and creating awareness for next time that topic comes up.

When you *do* get a response, remember Straight Line Sales and simply taking the next logical step.

If you get a response, you're back at a 1. A 10 on that straight line is not just receiving a single response, but instead, have a true back-and-forth conversation that you can take offline when it makes sense.

This cannot be done by bots. Bring in a human whose job is to have real conversations with people via direct messages.

4. Truth Is...**Building trust online is different.**

Let's take the human element one step further.

The ultimate reason someone is going to work with you is because they trust you.

Trust you to do what you say you're going to do.

Trust you to be the person who turns their stack of statements from various accounts into path for a better life.

Trust that you're going to do what's in their best interest.

Most advisors try to create that trust in their digital marketing and conversations through listing out their expertise, certifications, and services. And approximately 99.99999 percent of advisors' websites have something on it that talks about how much they care.

If that's you, great!

But just because you say it on your website doesn't mean your prospect will just take your word on it.

> You can't just tell people you're trustworthy.
> *You have to prove it.*

Because the truth is...Not every human or company is.

Even if they've made the appointment with you—virtually or in person—they're still not a client until checks are signed and money is moved.

Here are a couple of concepts that will make you more trustworthy as you convert those prospects at the bottom of the funnel.

Chapter 6

SPEED = TRUST:

There is a direct relationship between speed and trust.

The higher the trust is, the faster things happen.

The lower the trust is, the slower things happen.

And this relationship between speed and trust also correlates to costs and revenue.

☺ ↑ **SPEED** = ↑ TRUST ↓ COSTS

☹ ↓ **SPEED** = ↓ TRUST ↑ COSTS

For example…Before September 11, 2001, the idea of an airplane being hijacked and flown into the Twin Towers or the Pentagon was unfathomable. And therefore, getting through an airport was a breeze.

(Not that I can relate because I was in third grade when 2001 happened, but I did some research and man, as an avid traveler, getting to the airport a whopping thirty minutes before your flight sounds like a Disney movie).

What happened after 9/11? Trust went down, security went up, and you now have to get to the airport two hours before your flight, three if you're traveling internationally.

That's not a bad thing, of course. It's also unfathomable to think of a world where you could be on an airplane with somebody who has weapons, bombs, or pounds of drugs.

It's just the price we paid. Low trust, more time. And the airports had to pay a TON of money to create an environment where they can trust the people getting on a plane.

> Creating a *high-trust environment* for prospects will speed up (and increase) your conversion rates and lower your cost of doing business.

The faster you do the right things, especially the things you say you're going to do, the more people will trust you.

If you're taking your sweet time responding to emails or answering the phone, you're not helping the trust factor.

When we use processes and automations, this becomes less of an issue, but you still can't ignore the human element. Imagine if McDonald's assembly line was run by a bot. Not the same experience as having an automated process for taking orders, right?

But when you or another person on your team is involved in the bottom of funnel human touches, one of the biggest variables is *speed*.

When you get things done quickly, you're telling your audience that you are effective, experienced, and that you *care*.

To increase trust:

- → Make the calls, send the video emails, and respond to inquiries and messages fast
- → Send the meeting invite immediately
- → Be early for your virtual appointments
- → Have all the tabs and files already pulled up before the Zoom meeting so you aren't fumbling around (a.k.a. slowing the meeting down) trying to get your screen share to work

→ Send the video email within 24 hours of the interaction

→ Use overnight shipping for timely value-adds and packages

You know the saying; actions speak louder than words.

 LEADERSHIP HACK: Keep this in mind with your teams as well. There was a study done in 2017 about the impact of speed on a leader's effectiveness. The top 25 percent of leaders in terms of the speed at which they delivered and communicated with their team had more engaged employees and received more positive performance ratings than those who engaged with their team at a slower pace.

Nonverbal communications and environment matter

When you build a digital marketing funnel that is authentic and custom to your unique value proposition, your audience should feel like they already know you by the time they've reached the bottom of your funnel.

But no matter how you slice it, their first impression with you and your firm via direct, personal contact matters.

> In a digital world, the playing field for making a great first impression changes.

You can't look people straight in the eyes. You can't give a firm handshake or a hug. In person, a shaky first impression can be offset with other stimuli. For example, being able to offer them a cup of coffee. Having their favorite band's music playing in your reception area. Using Febreze to create a pleasant smell.

On the phone or on Zoom, all that goes out the window—but the importance of making a great first impression and having strong nonverbal communication remains. In fact, your non-verbal communication game needs to be even STRONGER in a virtual world.

If you're sending video emails, making phone calls, or engaging one-on-one with a prospect, remind yourself and your team about the power of non-verbal communication. For example:

Smile

You know the phrase—smiling and dialing.

Take this literally. Anyone making or taking calls should practice smiling before they answer the phone or call a prospect. Not fake smiles, real smiles. The ones where you get the crinkles in your eyes in addition to smiling with just your mouth.

The person on the other end will know immediately if the person on your firm's end is not smiling. And who wants to spend time with someone who doesn't seem happy to talk to them?

Do it on Zoom as well.

Posture

Obviously, your posture matters on Zoom, but it does when you're on the phone as well.

While making phone calls, stand up, put your shoulders back, and smile. Standing up, expanding your lungs, and walking or standing confidently may not feel like much to you, but the experience for the person on the other side is drastically different.

Watch Body Language and Framing

Hopefully, you've never had a police officer ask you to "put your hands where they can see them." But if you have, you know better than anyone how uncomfortable it can make someone when they can't see your hands.

With framing, you have to think within your computer screen. Very few people do.

In a virtual setting—either in video emails or in virtual meetings at the beginning of your sales process—people tend to do three things:

1. Sit REALLY FAR AWAY from the camera
2. Get all up in the face of the camera
3. Get close enough to the camera that people can see their face, but also far enough back that they can see the person's torso and hands

Be the third one.

And while we're at it...

Actively Listen

Lean in and tilt your head to show that you're listening. Nod your head at the right times. You're NOT multitasking.

Also, be mindful of how your gestures come across based on the listener's viewpoint. Are they distracting? Do they contradict what you're saying?

Your Environment Can Help Prove that You're Trustworthy

Someone at the bottom of your funnel is visualizing themselves working with you. Or at least trying to.

They've probably seen you or someone on your team's face, but what about your work environment?

I'm going to pretend for a second that I'm getting ready to hire a lawyer. For something cool, of course. And I'm stuck between two choices.

One has an outdated, cold, disorganized excuse for a workplace.

The other has a beautiful, modern office that is both clean and organized AND warm and inviting.

The second option is *immediately* more trustworthy.

Even if you're a virtual advisor, the environment where you conduct your meetings matters to your prospect.

You can burn all the trust generated by the *best digital marketing in the world* to the ground in an *instant* if your prospect glimpses a workspace that puts your credibility at risk.

Hiring a staging professional or getting a consultation on lighting, decor, office setup, and flow is priceless.

Once you've done this, show it off. Lean into it. Put pictures of your office on your website. Record a video tour of your office that tells a personal story. Record another video with directions to your office, where to park, which door to enter, and what to expect when they show up and send it alongside your scheduling link and as an immediate follow up to any booked appointments.

Besides making you more trustworthy, you'll help your soon-to-be-client visualize coming into your office and working with you *while* minimizing any objections related to getting to, parking at, and finding a place they've never been before.

 CLIENT EXPERIENCE HACK: While we're at it, do yourself and your prospects a favor and send them written and/or instructions on how to use Zoom (or whatever virtual meeting tool you use) when it is booked, and include it again in the appointment reminders.

Chapter 6

Materializing the relationship and turning the prospects that come from your online efforts into clients is all about specializing in how you connect as humans and creating an environment of trust in your interactions from afar—long before you connect in person.

Next Steps & Resources You Can Use *Today*

To access the notes from an intimate and exclusive Triad Partners Community Call with John Ruhlin about the art of gifting, head to: www.truthaboutdm.com/gifting

If you like the idea of handwritten notes, but don't have the time to use them as often as you'd like, check out my favorite tool for systematizing and scaling handwritten notes here: www.truthaboutdm.com/handwrittennotes

Chapter 7

The Art of Addressing Your Audience

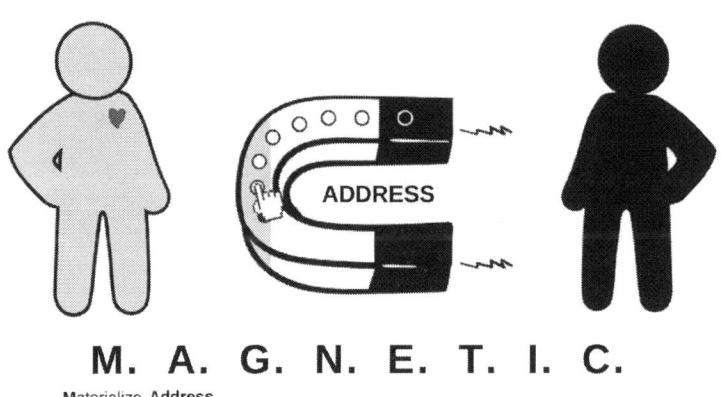

M. A. G. N. E. T. I. C.
Materialize **Address**

You've got formulas and guidelines for how you build financial plans, right?

Well marketers have formulas for content, the words, videos, social posts and other collateral that bring people into their funnels using the digital written word by addressing their audience, their issues, and their goals.

They know how use language online to capture and keep attention, create connections, and get people to engage.

Basically, they crush it at copywriting.

Often, when one hears "copywriting," or writing "copy", their mind goes straight to intellectual property.

In your marketing, especially online, copywriting is basically "marketing industry jargon" for the written word.

Thankfully, their formulas for doing this are not rocket science and can be replicated in any industry, including ours. And, once you've defined your audience and their unique goals/challenges, this trio of knowledge will get them where you need them. So, let's check out how to:

1. Write captivating headlines
2. Write short and long copy (and when to do each)
3. Make your content standout
4. Create impossible to pass up CTAs
5. Take advantage of copywriting formulas so you aren't constantly recreating the wheel

This chapter is about leveraging the online written word to address your audience in a way that keeps them motivated, engaged, and drives results.

1. Truth Is…**Headlines need to be interesting enough to compete with… Everything.**

Headlines are what you see when you're scrolling through various news sites. The sole purpose of a headline is to draw someone into your content.

Journalists are some of the best at crafting headlines because they *get your attention*. Check out some of these recent ones:

"Woman wins $10 million after accidentally pushing the wrong button on lottery machine"

"For Valentine's Day, the Bronx Zoo lets you name a roach after your sweetheart"

"Droughts Push Farmers Toward Water Witches"

In the digital marketing world, your headline is the first thing people see in your posts on social media, on your website, in your webinars, in your ads, in emails, or on blogs.

People scan your headlines first to determine if they want to keep reading what you have to say.

World-renowned copy expert David Oglby said it best: *"On average, five times as many people read the headlines as the body copy. When you have written your headline, you have spent 80 cents out of your dollar."*

A headline should make people **stop scrolling,** raise their hand, and say, "Wait, they're talking to me. I should pay attention to this."

A powerful headline has two things: An attention grabber, and a hook point. A hook point is a statement that elicits an emotional response by your audience.

Here are some examples:

- *"If You Are a Texan Getting Ready to Retire: Uncle Sam's Coming."*
- *"Attention 62-Year-Olds: Don't Make This Mistake When Claiming Social Security."*
- *"Are You a Self-Minted Millionaire? What Are You Doing to Protect Your Privacy?"*

You'll notice that each of these headlines start by calling out *exactly* who they're talking to.

Here are a couple other essential qualities of irresistible and attention-grabbing headlines:

- Creates curiosity
- Creates a fear of missing out FOMO
- Promises a result
- Is a cliffhanger
- Creates contrast

At the end of this chapter, there's an opportunity to grab a list of examples you can begin using today. Don't miss it.

2. Truth Is...**If you don't master copywriting, its game over.**

You've grabbed your audience's attention with a killer headline. Now what?

We use copywriting to expand on the message, deliver value, tell the story, and engage them further.

Copywriting is an art and a skill. It is arguably the backbone of your entire digital marketing machine, and when it's effective *and relevant*, it gets people to pay enough attention to your message that they take action.

Powerful copy evokes an emotional response, grabs attention, and creates results.

> Having a killer copywriter on your team is priceless.

At the *bare minimum*, you need to understand how copy works when you evaluate potential digital marketing partners. It's not as difficult as you might think.

The Difference Between Short and Long Form Copy

There are two types of copy: Short form and long form.

How and when you use the two types depend on:

- The context of the copy
- How much your audience knows prior to reading it
- The intent of your message

Short form is very concise and written for quick, powerful *impact*. They're the messages that are typically less than 1,000 words and always get straight to the point.

Believe it or not, short form copy is WAY harder to do than you might think. It requires no-nonsense, no-fluff language that captures attention and creates influence with precision.

Short form copy is used in your marketing machine where the stakes are low or as a springboard for longer form copy. For example, it:

- ✓ Prompts prospects to click through to learn more
- ✓ Encourages your audience to clear low hurdles like signing up for your email newsletter, reading a blog, downloading a lead magnet
- ✓ Tells a greater story with media-rich content, like pictures or videos

Short form is very concise and written to be memorable and impactful. It gets straight to the point: *"Here's the situation and here's the next step."*

If you get too wordy in a message around an easy action, your audience may feel like they don't need to move forward because they already have enough information.

Save your longer messages for the higher ticket items, complex topics, and actions that require larger commitments.

This is where long form copy comes in.

Long Form Copy

Long form copy, often referred to as a sales letter, should be used to tell a story, persuade, and address the many objections the public has about giving a financial advisor an inch.

Usually, marketers use long form copy when they're offering:

- Something expensive
- A specialty or unusual product or service
- A product or service that most people don't think they need

Guess what? Financial planning, especially financial planning for a niche, fits all three of those criteria.

I wouldn't recommend long form copy in ALL your online messages—especially in your top of funnel content—but your value proposition isn't exactly the same as Yankee Candle's. It's a lot more complicated for you than, *"Our candles make everything smell good and you should spend $25 on one just like all your friends."*

You need to be able to tell a story that relates to a pain point, paint a picture of the outcome the audience desires and has an emotional attachment to, and proactively address any questions along the way.

Therefore, you'll want to have someone on your team who is good at writing concise, yet comprehensive and persuasive messages.

Don't worry about the *specific* length. Just make sure every word, phrase, or idea you're communicating has purpose. **If you're connecting, adding value, and creating engagement, length is a non-issue.**

The people outside of your ideal audience might not read the entire thing, but that's fine. In fact, if your copy is on point but they don't stick around long enough to read your entire message, it's either not relevant or they aren't ready for your offer. In those cases, we didn't want them to read it anyways. Snaps to them for self-disqualifying.

Now…

Do not confuse "long form copy" with "so long it's *painful to read.*"

We've all read the blog or article that just goes on and on before getting to the point.

For example, it drives me absolutely insane when I Google a recipe for a cocktail (my husband Joe is the cook of the family, I'm the bartender) and the blog starts off with six paragraphs about why the author was craving the drink and how many red lights they hit on the way to buy the ingredients and what color socks they wore when they made it. I don't know why they all do that. Drives me freakin' nuts.

Don't be that guy. Not only are you doing yourself a disservice, but you're essentially disrespecting your audience's time. They'll go straight to the next advisor who gets to the point.

Use your long form copy:

- ✓ In the absence of videos and images
- ✓ When prompting your audience to jump over higher hurdles that require more time and energy on their part
- ✓ When you're asking prospects to provide more than their basic contact information—especially specific info about their finances

3. Truth Is...**It's a hurdle to get your audience to read your copy at all. Make it scannable.**

Use bullet points to make your long form copy more scannable and concise.

Choose this:

There are two types of copy.

Both have a place in your marketing.

Each can make or break your content.

Over:

There are two types of copy, both of which have a role in your marketing messaging and have the potential to either make or break the success and effectiveness of your digital content.

Which one was easier to read?

Using scannable copy is not just marketing philosophy—it's a science. In fact, the Nielsen Norman Group (NN Group), a world leader in user-based research, proved it.

The NN Group conducted a series of eye tracking studies over twenty-three plus years to better understand how people read online.

Here's what they found:

- People do not read online, they *scan*
- The way people's eyes travel across pages/the way they consume the information is not necessarily linear, meaning line for line

Chapter 7

- These consistencies about how people read online are universal behaviors that are consistent amongst various languages and cultures

Year after year, these findings have remained the same.

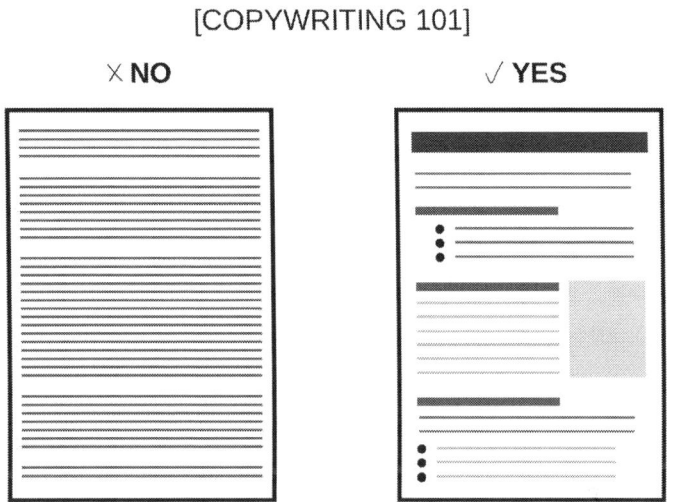

Based on the science of how people read (and don't read) online, there are five things to accomplish when writing any form of copy:

➔ **1. Use clear and bold headings and subheadings** to break up your content and make it easy for readers to scan.

➔ **2. Frontload your content.** Make your statements of impact and value closer to the left side of the page and towards the beginning of any message—not the end

➔ **3. Use bullet points, bolded text, underlines, and other formatting techniques** to draw attention to the key points

➔ **4. Use basic language.** Your copy must be easy to read— if someone has to reread a sentence because they didn't understand it the first time or they're wondering what a word means, you've already lost

→ **5. Look for opportunities to use visuals.** Whether it's a graphic on a blog or an emoji in a post, you're breaking up the text, enhancing the message, and making your content easier to digest

If You're an Advisor Writing Copy, Dumb it Down

Of those five guidelines, the one advisors need to work hard at is No. 4—keep things clear and concise. Despite your urge to use (or difficulties avoiding) industry jargon, aim to keep your copy at a kindergarten level.

> You can't sell complex with complex.

If someone is going to take time away from TikTok or their kids or whatever they're binging on Netflix to hear what you have to say, do your part to make it worthwhile.

Which, in the case of "using plain language," means: Make thinking about money less painful than it already may be and ensure that reading your posts or emails doesn't feel like work.

One way to make sure your copy is *readable* is to read your copy out loud—or even better—start by recording yourself, have it transcribed, and then use that as the foundation for your copy.

This allows you to use your natural language. If you talk to your audience the way you would talk to a friend, you become more relatable.

If that isn't enough, it will make you more *trustworthy*—a.k.a. the name of the game.

People can't relate to big words they don't understand and over-engineered responses. **And even if you've captured their attention, they're a lot less likely to believe you if they can't understand you.**

Chapter 7

Use your natural language. Talk to your consumer audience the way you would talk to a friend.

Good copy is less about perfect grammar and more about creating an *experience* that feels like communicating with someone you like and trust.

4. Truth Is...**Calls to Action (CTAs) are the icing on the cake.**

If you want more followers, a bigger email list, more attendees at your workshop, more people to listen to your podcast — it won't happen in a meaningful way without a good call to action, or CTA.

Even if you *nailed* the headline and copy.

A CTA gives your audience a nudge to take the action you want them to take.

Without CTAs, people are a lot less likely to take the next step, and therefore, your audience's process through your funnel will become stagnant.

"YOUR CALL TO ACTION NEEDS TO BE STRONGER. IT'S MORE LIKE A WHISPER TO ACTION."

Strong CTAs are:

- Short and concise
- Benefit-oriented
- Action-oriented
- Easy to see
- Easy to do
- Not too pushy
- Compelling and create urgency

Now a couple of recommendations on your CTAs:

Tell 'Em, Tell 'Em, Tell 'Em

It feels like common sense to have the CTA at the end of your message, but I strongly recommend you have several prompts to take that desired action throughout your message.

Tell 'em what you're going to tell them. Tell 'em what you gotta tell them. Tell 'em what you told them.

Apply this same principle to how to you introduce, present, and remind your audience what the next step is.

> It is an egregious mistake to assume that you're going to hold 100 percent of your audience's attention until the end of every message.

Most people will not watch your video all the way until the end, read your entire blog, or check out every corner of your website.

Your benefit-oriented CTA should be clearly presented as soon as possible so those with even the *shortest* attention span won't miss it.

Note: Use your common sense to avoid going overboard or ask a friend if you've crossed the line between "direct, benefit-oriented nudges" and straight up nagging.

Make your CTAs impossible to miss

It's not just about the words we use. The ways we *visually* position our CTAs have a major impact on their effectiveness.

Remember: People DON'T READ online. They scan.

Here are a couple of examples of how to do this with various pieces of content:

CTAs in Videos:

- → Add graphics that spell out the next step and desired action
- → Deliver the CTA and provide direction on how to do so in the video's description or in the social media post

CTAs in Written Content (website copy, emails, etc):

- → Make the text stand out using bold, underline, and/or italics. You want it to *look* clickable
- → Use blue—people are used to seeing links and additional content in blue

CTAs on Landing Pages or Websites:

- → Literally make the CTA look like a button. Make sure it's clear that it's something to click
- → Use pictures of people looking toward the CTA button
- → Use colors that stand out from the rest of your page or contrasting colors in general
- → Surround the button or the call to action by white space

PSYCHOLOGY HACK: Although you, your team, and your vendors should be testing your CTA's, studies show that buttons with rounded corners (like the first example above) draw people's eyes inward—a.k.a. to the CTA on the button.

SAMPLE CTA BUTTON

AND HERE'S ANOTHER

5. Truth Is...**Formulas make copy writing easy.**

Here's what the Headline + Copy + CTA combination looks like when applied to proven formulas, which I'll show you in a sec, to both short and long form copy.

For the sake of giving easy examples, I'm going to use relatively general topics. When you identify your niche, it'll be a lot easier to dial these in.

Short Form Example:

Here's a sample short form copywriting formula: **Problem + Agitate + Solve**

Problem (Headline): You can't avoid paying taxes.

Agitate: Today's tax rates are at historic lows.

Solve (CTA): Watch the quick, straightforward video below to access the three biggest tax opportunities today to lower your retirement tax bracket for years to come.

Long Form Example:

Here's another powerful formula to use in your long form copy:

Problem + Agitate + Here's What Happens If You *Don't* Solve It + Here's What Happens If You *Do* + Solve.

Problem (Headline):

Going through a divorce is one of the most difficult life transitions you'll ever experience.

Do we want the transition to be quick and amicable? ABSOLUTELY.

But can we count on it? Sadly, no.

Every single decision you make is on emotional steroids.

And, when it's all said and done…

Making sure you got your fair share and have financial stability will make a big difference in what your next new chapter looks like.

Agitate:

Most people find themselves both shocked and overwhelmed about the number of decisions that need to be made.

Who gets the furniture?

What do you actually own?

Which holidays do you get the kids or grandkids?

How does health insurance work?

Who gets the pension?

Where does the divorce leave the retirement assets?

The list goes on.

Here's what happens if you don't solve it:

Basically, you have two options.

The first? Do it alone.

But in my 25 years of experience…

The women who do it alone have a much harder time than it already is.

Poor, rash decisions are made. They lose themselves. Their emotional and physical health suffers.

More often than not, they walk away without the financial stability they need to support their next chapter.

Here's what happens if you do (get help and make good decisions):

The alternative is getting support.

Emotional, physical, and—most importantly—financial help.

Working with a financial advisor who specializes in divorce will guide you through every decision, big or small.

Working with a trusted fiduciary can prevent you from making emotionally charged decisions around the foundation for your future: Your money.

Solve (CTA):

Join us next Tuesday alongside other women facing the EXACT same decisions you're facing today and learn the 10 Steps of Protecting What's Yours During Divorce.

Click the link below to save your seat at this uniquely empowering and informative experience.

…You see how much easier this gets when you use a formula?

What I want you to take note of in each of those examples is how they **address:**

- The specific part of their audience the message is intended for
- Their paint points, goals, and the potential of solving the problem
- The benefits of solving the problem—and exactly how to take that next step

Super easy to do when you're crystal clear on the one thing you are laser-focused on helping your specific audience solve.

Learning the art of copywriting and **addressing** your audience via the digitally written word is an essential, technical skill—not only in the future, but today. We all know how messages can get misconstrued when you send a text instead of picking up the phone. How an in-person interaction is much richer than one virtually.

Only those that can communicate clearly online and master copywriting will survive.

Next Steps & Resources You Can Use *Today*

To take advantage of 25 formulas for crafting attention-grabbing headlines (as opposed to regularly reinventing the wheel), head to: www.truthaboutdm.com/headlines

If you'd love to see another go-to copywriting formula in action used by a high performing advisor (plus 18 *additional formulas* you can use), grab it at: www.truthaboutdm.com/copywriting

Chapter 8

Gains for Your Audience, Gains for You

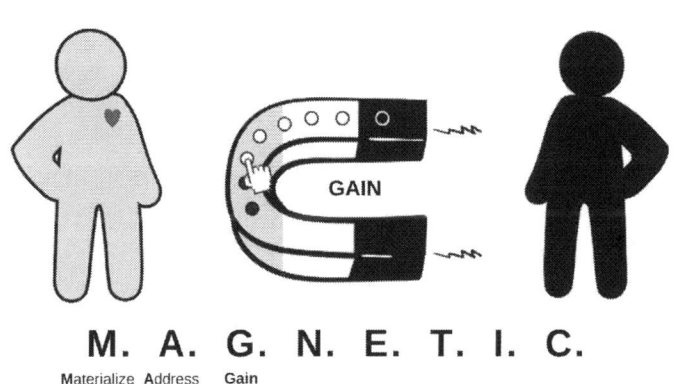

M. A. G. N. E. T. I. C.
Materialize Address **Gain**

As we know, appointments with warm, qualified prospects in our ideal audience don't fall out of the sky.

For this to happen, you need to focus on creating massive value that allows you to gather leads and capture insights about where someone might be in your funnel based on how they engage with you digitally.

As we know, based on The CAVE Conversion Formula™, adding value is the meat of it.

When you deliver a boatload of value, you create a desire to learn more about working together and a ton of opportunities to gather the info of qualified, interested people along the way.

Some advisors charge for live events, seminars, or online courses. Advisors who charge for a first meeting spend more time with motivated, ideal clients by creating a barrier to entry.

But to keep it simple, not only for you but also your team, let's just focus on getting prospects to buy *you*.

The way to do it? Give your prospects and audience ALLLL of your *best* information, hacks, tips, stories, and education away before they become clients.

While you're helping your audience *gain* the knowledge and empowerment to solve their problems and bring the vision for their future to life, you'll gain names, their contact information, and ultimately, new ideal prospects in your funnel.

Everybody wins! And to make sure reading this chapter is another W, I'm going to lay out:

1. How to not only build, but safeguard, your online leads—regardless of what happens to the digital landscape
2. What it looks like to add value to your audience while enticing them to move further down your funnel
3. Examples of various lead magnets, broken down by top, middle, and bottom of funnel
4. A key digital marketing asset that most advisors aren't properly leveraging—and ultimately helps you build your list

Chapter 8

1. Truth Is...**If it's free, people are more likely to want it.**

Having and giving away free, valuable stuff is a powerful and research-based psychological tool for attracting people to your content and value proposition.

People LOVE free stuff.

There's a behavioral economics term for how much harder it is to resist something that's free: The Zero Price Effect.

The Zero Price Effect, defined by economist, author, and Professor at Duke University, Dan Ariely, suggests that there's a *higher perceived benefit of things that are free.*

Ariely conducted an experiment published by MIT confirming this. The study offered a study group the choice between two types of chocolates (Hershey's—a lower quality chocolate, and Ferrero Rocher—a high quality chocolate) at three different price points.

When the Hershey's was free, the demand increased and the demand for the Ferrero went down *substantially*. In the other two price choices, the differences in demand were almost undetectable.

This may seem insignificant, but in further studies conducted by Ariely, evidence supporting the Zero Price Effect is consistent when there are both higher prices and stakes.

People chose a free $10 Amazon gift card over a $20 Amazon that was offered at $13.

During another study, when a tattoo was offered for free, there were lines to get the ink at the tattoo parlor. 65 percent of those who were waiting in line reported that they *wouldn't* get the tattoo if it wasn't free.

Monetarily free pieces of value are an important piece of the puzzle (despite the very real exchange that occurs when you're asking for time, information, and attention).

The idea is to make people feel like you're giving away something amazing at a MINIMAL cost.

2. Truth Is...**Lead magnets build your database and get you closer to close.**

As we know, it's unlikely that people will commit to working with you without seeing if some of your lower commitment offerings hold any merit or are relevant/valuable to your audience.

Although gathering someone's contact information is not the equivalent of booking an appointment, for every person's contact info you gather, you build a larger group of people in your database who are one step closer to the end goal.

Chapter 8

Before I jump right into examples of the lead magnets you can use, let's quickly look at what they are and how they help you. Lead magnets:

- ✓ Add value
- ✓ Use micro-offers to attract your ideal audience so that you can build a relationship that leads to the ultimate offer
- ✓ Get people to raise their hand and enthusiastically jump into your funnel

The basic—and official—definition of a lead magnet is a free value-add that is offered in exchange for someone's contact information. Simplified, this means using value to gather leads and help prospects progress in your funnel.

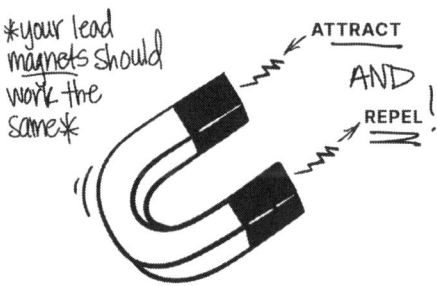

As social media platforms move in and out of favor and algorithms change, you want to own your audience. Day in and day out, one of your biggest focuses is to build your contact list, email list, text list, and leads list.

Your lead magnet is the incentive for your audience that allows you to build a list that is *yours.*

An effective lead magnet is a strategic, purposeful value-add that creates a specific, positive outcome or solves a pain point for your audience.

And, no, the opt-in for your monthly market summary e-blast offered on your website is *not* the fastest path to success.

Make sure they know it's free!

In the spirit of the Zero Price Effect, let's remind prospects that whatever value you're offering is free.[7]

Think about the perception of our industry. Unfortunately, people rarely have an accurate perception of "the cost" of working with a financial advisor.

As more advisors emerge with a value proposition of being "fee-only" or "fee-based" (versus commission-based via product sales), the industry is collectively telling people to pay attention to fees.

Uncovering fees and unnecessary charges are also ways that advisors sell against each other and move money to their firm during a *complimentary portfolio review*.

Raise your hand if you've ever said, *"This person is charging you X in annual fees. If you move your money to me, I may be able to create more value AND lower your fees."*

No judgement. If you can lower client fees (ethically and transparently), do it.

 PROCEED WITH CAUTION: Although lowering client fees is a value-add, training your audience to be HYPER fee-sensitive by making your comp structure your primary value proposition isn't super smart. If the thing that "sells" them is your super low fees, they'll pay attention when someone else comes around with even lower fees. Getting people too attached to numbers, in general, is not the move. Focus on outcomes and achievements, not bps and benchmarks.

But we have an industry-wide problem here. The public doesn't have a reliable point of reference for an acceptable cost to work with an advisor because there's no industry-wide standardized approach.

We can't assume that people know what's free and what isn't.

In the headlines and copy related to your lead magnets—and when its relevant—use language like:

- Complimentary
- No obligation
- No cost

Your lead magnets must be absolutely irresistible

You want people to see what you're offering and STOP whatever they're doing, abandon their fear of subscribing to *another* list, and get them excited to hand over their beloved cell phone number or email address to get it.

It has to be relevant. Convenient to access. Easy to digest.

So good that once they receive it, they wonder why you aren't charging for the amount of value you're providing to strangers on the Internet.

In most industries, "written" content is the best performing lead magnet. Think eBook or whitepaper.

In financial services, things are a little different. In our industry, written content falls to the bottom of the list. This shouldn't be that surprising. What normal person outside of our industry wants to read an eBook about taxes? Not many.

Instead, prioritize *visually rich content*, like videos and images.

Why use more complex words to talk about this pie in the sky thing that is people's MONEY when we can lean into videos and images that make our lead magnets more accessible, memorable, interesting, and create emotional connections?

Ensure you have high-value lead magnets in prominent spaces anywhere an ideal client may encounter your firm's value proposition online.

Having various versions of these value-adds throughout your funnel that solve a massive problem is where a good campaign starts and ends.

3. Truth Is...**There are thousands of ways you can gather leads by creating prospect "gains" throughout your funnel.**

Here are three interesting lead magnet strategies used in other industries that, when combined with your expertise, focused audience, and voice, are going to give you an edge in The Attention Economy.

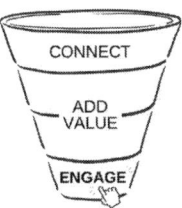

Bottom of Funnel Lead Magnet: A Plan Overview & Case Study

People want to know exactly what they're going to walk away with when they work with you. Not the easiest to do in our industry in a tangible way. You cannot test, taste, sample, or try on a Roth conversion.

But you can showcase a sample financial plan.

I'm not talking about a PDF full of illustrations and eMoney reports. I'm talking about your packaged, proprietary deliverable that creates an idea of what they uniquely receive from your firm.

It should *not* get into the weeds, but instead, additionally function as a case study for your ideal clients. It should highlight the pain points, problems solved, and what becomes possible if you work together.

In that sample, make sure you highlight how the review creates actionable insights that make a difference.

Even better, include a sample fact finder that was used in the construction of the plan. Why? Because people want to know what they're getting into. And you can paint a picture of how you're different based on the way you approach getting to know your client and their goals.

CTA/HEADLINE EXAMPLE: *"Preview Exactly How We Approach Solving These Problems for These People in Our Named Process™"*

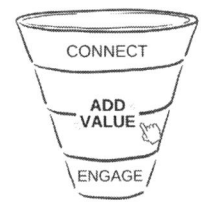

Middle of Funnel Lead Magnet: Podcasts and Audiobooks

Audio content is incredibly easy to consume. Unlike videos or written content, they allow your audience to engage with your firm while they are multitasking and doing other things. Think about it: People can't watch a video or read an eBook while they're driving their car, cleaning their house, lifting weights.

As our world gets busier, it gives you a bit more wiggle room on the specificity of the audio books' value because, in a sense, it casts a wider net by not eliminating the people that are too busy to sit and read printed literature.

Plus, the path to the brain is faster with audio, through the ears, than visually, through the eyes.

The best part? Your prospect gets to spend TIME with you and hear your voice while they live their life in familiar places and around familiar faces. The intimacy here, especially at a distance, is hard to match.

 HAVE A PODCAST? While we're here, and because I've heard so many advisors say that they've never gotten much traction from their show, here's a quick strategy. Not only is the show itself a lead magnet, but you can create a landing page for each episode offering downloadable show notes or unique offers related to the show. It's great that they're listening—even better if you know they're listening.

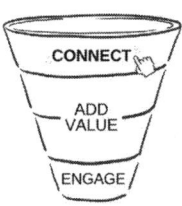 *Top of Funnel Lead Magnet: eBooks*

I know eBooks will continue to be something advisors use, so instead of avoiding written lead magnets entirely, I want to give you some ideas on how to make them work.

If your eBook is specific enough to solve a very specific problem for a very specific type of person, this isn't an issue. Your eBook shouldn't be too vague or general otherwise, people won't be super inclined to sign up for the equivalent of a homework assignment.

Additionally, you want to counteract the perceived effort it might take to read your eBook by:

- → Promising those who pursue your eBook with at least one quick win they'll walk away with
- → Setting expectations and painting a picture about why your eBook won't be painful using a solid headline
- → Choosing topics that your target market will enjoy

→ Getting away from thinking this type of content needs to be as big as a book (although the value inside should be a whole book's worth)! A smaller guide is much more effective

P.S. Can we stop calling them "eBooks" and get a little creative here? Even if you've got a killer eBook, if someone has been disappointed by a lackluster eBook from another advisor, they may see the word "eBook", associate it with another firm who is now spamming their email inbox, and keep scrolling. Depending on the content, ask yourself if there's another word you can use that's a bit more interesting and benefit-oriented.

CTA/HEADLINE EXAMPLE: *"Access A COMPLIMENTARY THREE PAGE GUIDE That Contains Every Single Thing You Need To Know About Relocating in Retirement."*

4. Truth Is...**Lead magnets benefit your audience. Landing pages benefit you.**

There is a ton of value for your audience when you've got a solid lead magnet game.

Landing pages are a vehicle for delivering your valuable lead magnet and create the value for *you*. They're an essential part of driving conversions.

> Landing pages have one job and one job only:
> *Capturing leads.*

Any webpage that you send visitors to where you're highlighting an opportunity to enter your funnel or encouraging them to take a specific step is a landing page.

While landing pages might look and feel like a website, they are a completely different animal in appearance, capability, and functionality.

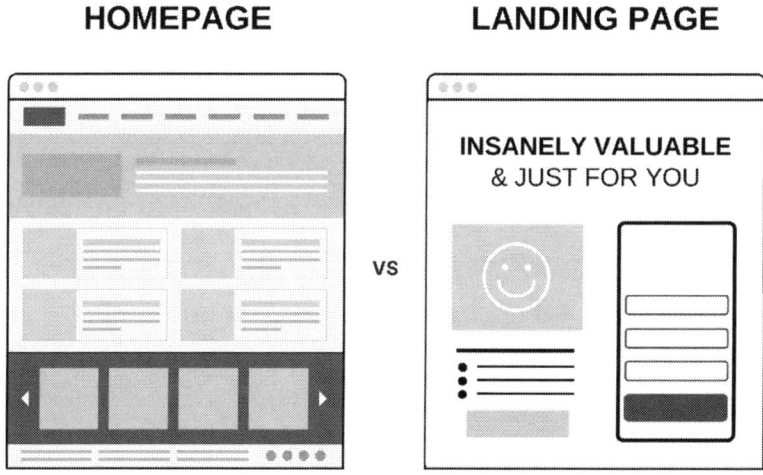

Websites are much more complex than landing pages. Your website is where people can click around, read your bio, learn about your services, check out your blog, whatever.

The landing page is much more strategic, simple, and has one purpose: To get viewers to take one very specific action.

Unlike a website, landing pages don't have any other places for visitors to get lost, forget the reason they went to the page, and jump ship. Simplicity on your landing pages will make it easy for your audience to take that next step.

Landing page strategy is literally as simple as:

1. "Hey, here's this value that you need"
2. "Give me your information to get it"

Chapter 8

Ok, fine. It's not exactly that simple. The simplicity, or complexity, of your landing page will vary depending on (you guessed it!) where the prospect is in your funnel.

But, regardless of the purpose or format of your landing page, they all have one thing in common: the "fold".

Digital marketers will use the terms *"above the fold"* and *"below the fold"* in reference to the two primary pieces of a landing page.

"Above the fold" means the top part of your landing page that greets visitors and the content they see without having to scroll down.

Anything "below the fold" simply means the audience has to scroll to see it.

In other words, **the space above the fold is the most important real-estate on your landing page.**

The goal of the landing page is to capture their information, but you have capture and keep their attention first.

Here are the key components to include and optimize above the fold:

The Headline

The headline on a landing page shows up like a CTA. Use a concise, attention-grabber that:

- Tells your audience they're in the right place
- Leads people to act by using action-oriented words or time-based language like "today" or "now"

Getting your audience to take action starts at the top.

Hero Content

Digital marketers use the term "hero content" to refer to a compelling picture or video that reinforces that accessing your content will make their life better.

When you're offering a deliverable or download, the hero content should be a visual preview of the offer. For example, if it's an eBook, it's a picture of the eBook. This helps make your offer tangible and create trust by saying, "Look! This is a real thing!"

When you're offering value for something that requires a bigger commitment of time, trust, or effort like an event registration or scheduling a consultation, consider using a video for your hero content and put that bad boy front and center.

A quick note on this. When you use a video as the hero content on a landing page, you will want to shorten the rest of the written copy on the page to avoid distractions and make sure that video gets watched.

The Form

Your form is where the rubber hits the road. It's where the action happens. This is where the prospect gives you their contact information and permission to further the relationship. Getting your forms right is crucial.

Financial services has the fourth highest form abandonment rate meaning that *75.7%(!)* of forms in our industry never get completed.

When you're considering which fields should be required, think about what is absolutely necessary for the conversion to take place, what information you can gather later down the road, and if the information you're asking actually helps you better serve the prospect.

Your form cannot be complicated, frustrating, or create any doubt that the action is safe and beneficial.

Losing a conversion means losing the potential for a relationship with that potential client.

There are four primary reasons people abandon forms:

1. *Security concerns: 29 percent*

Security concerns ultimately come down to trust. You'll want to clarify that their information is safe. Asking for overly sensitive information can create friction in your audience's mind when they ask themselves if this is a trustworthy, a.k.a. safe, action for them to take.

2. *Form was too long: 27 percent*

Be very clear and concise in telling your audience how you'll be using their information and what happens next.

The form itself will vary depending on the type of offer and who it's intended for. For example, if the form leads to a simple download, only ask for their name and email address. If it's an event registration, you'll want to collect more information, like a good phone number (ideally cell phone) and an optional prompt to gain insights on what they want to get out of the event.

If you really need their address, make a note in conversational language about how you'll be using it to send them something relevant and valuable in the mail.

If you must have that phone number, let them know the value of, purpose, and frequency of communications they'll receive.

As a general rule, the fewer fields in your form, the better.

1. *Advertisements or upselling: 11 percent*

CAVE does not stand for Coerce, Aggressive, Veil (your Intentions), Embellish. LOL I know that's corny, but forreal. Point is, there is no room, ever, to be pushy, embellish the truth, or be more focused on ourselves that our audience when we ask them to share information. Agreed? Agreed.

2. *Unclear reason for collecting information: 10 percent*

Above the form, you'll want a headline, information on the benefits that encourages your audience to fill it out and hit submit, as well as set expectations of what happens once their info's submitted.

The button on the form is—you guessed it—a CTA. *"Submit to Gain This," "Click Here to Book," "Save Your Seat," etc.*

Reminder, it should literally look like a button.

 QUICK HACK FOR YOUR CTA'S: Studies repeatedly show that the best color to use on a CTA button is orange. Definitely test the colors and think outside the box to create contrast in those colors, but orange is consistently a color at the top of the list.

Use Strong Copy to Keep them Motivated and Create Conversions

Let's say your prospect clicks over to your landing page, sees the form, but isn't sure if they want to fill it out. Motivate that audience by attention grabbing subheadings and feature simple, scannable copy that illustrates the transformation your client might experience by having access to this lead magnet.

Whether you use short or long form copy will depend on the offer on the landing page. For a simple lead magnet, don't overwhelm your audience with a manuscript about the value-add.

Just the quick bullet points on the promises and benefits of the lead magnet should do it.

When it's a larger commitment ask—like signing up for an event or a consultation—you'll want to include messages that display transparency and overcome objections that someone may have about signing up, in addition to painting a picture of the problems that signing up can solve. Just make sure it's scannable.

How to Create Trust on your Landing Pages Below the Fold

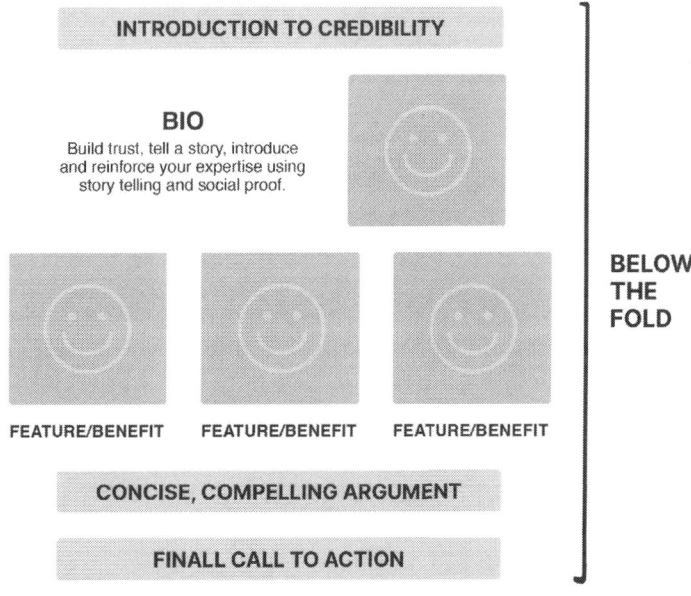

Lay Off the Stock Images

Of all places where you don't want to use stock images when you're driving conversions from people who are ready to take the next step by committing to going deeper with you, this is it.

If any outside industry expert studied how advisors show up online, one of the first things they'd get rid of is stock images. Our industry, thanks to all the cookie cutter templates, uses way too many tacky, anti-trustworthy stock images.

Using images, videos, and graphics on your landing pages to create trust through authenticity is crucial. It helps you set the stage for your audience opting in or booking.

In a generic campaign absent of personal stories and convictions and full of stock images and canned content, the landing pages and copy naturally look, smell, and feel like a pitch. And that's really all they are.

Eliminate the use of stock images everywhere you can. Not just on your landing pages, but *anywhere you show up online.*

When you lose the stock images (and stock pitches), you're building deeper *relationships* with your audience. Pictures of real people—pictures of YOUR face—that they can relate to and connect with completely flips the dynamic.

The story is easier to tell. It comes from the heart, its laser-focused and ultimately…

You become less reliant on a ton of traffic because when there's a greater connection, there are more conversions.

Use Testimonials (or Find a Workaround!)

Landing pages are one of the most crucial places to have a strong testimonial in your middle or bottom of funnel content. People trust other people, remember?

If you're reading this book, you're probably in the industry. And you probably think I'm crazy for saying to use testimonials. I'd do the same.

The key point here is that…In any other industry, your audience is used seeing testimonials on landing pages. They're subconsciously trained to look for them.

Are testimonials allowed in our industry? Yes and no. The testimonial landscape is currently too complex, not where it should be, and I don't see that changing soon.

It's a problem that we can't solve here today.

I know most of you can't use testimonials right now—or atleast with confidence. But it doesn't make the need for credibility and social proof go away.

Ever been featured in a major publication, radio station, media outlet? Throw that logo on your landing page. Also, add the logos for your certifications and find visual representations of why you're trustworthy.

I'll talk more about other potential workarounds for testimonials and creating social proof in Chapter 10 and Chapter 13, but for now, just know what you're up against.

Ask yourself: *"Knowing what I know about how I can/cannot use testimonials, understanding what people look for online to get affirmation before taking action/purchasing, and being realistic about industry sentiment...How can I work with what I've got to create trust?"*

Give Them a Chance to Connect With You

Bios are another way to introduce credibility and create connections.

Use the bio on your landing page to affirm and create trust in the human behind the form who is collecting their information.

Some marketing companies include advisor's bios from their website along with a picture here. Most don't.

I want you to take that a step further.

In your bio, talk in first person and tell a story directly to whoever is on your landing page. Make it more like a personal letter directly from you that shares your heart alongside your credentials.

Even better? Use a video.

5. Truth Is...**Landing pages are built with the end in mind.**

Because capturing a lead's information is not the end goal, use what's called a "Thank You Page" to immediately prompt your audience with another opportunity to progress in your funnel.

For example—When someone submits their name, email, or phone number to receive your free eBook, they should be taken to a landing page that thanks them, lets them know that the free report is on the way, and prompts them to opt-in and listen to your podcast or watch your webinar.

Another example—When someone registers for an event or a seminar, use your Thank You Page to prompt them to download materials that will be valuable and relevant to the event, or even better, provide an option to skip the event and schedule a consultation to get their specific questions answered.

A Thank You Page is basically a second landing page that follows the first landing page.

Once someone converts on the original landing page, use a Thank You Page to present the next hurdle on the straight line, give them another way to engage, and/or get them to take action.

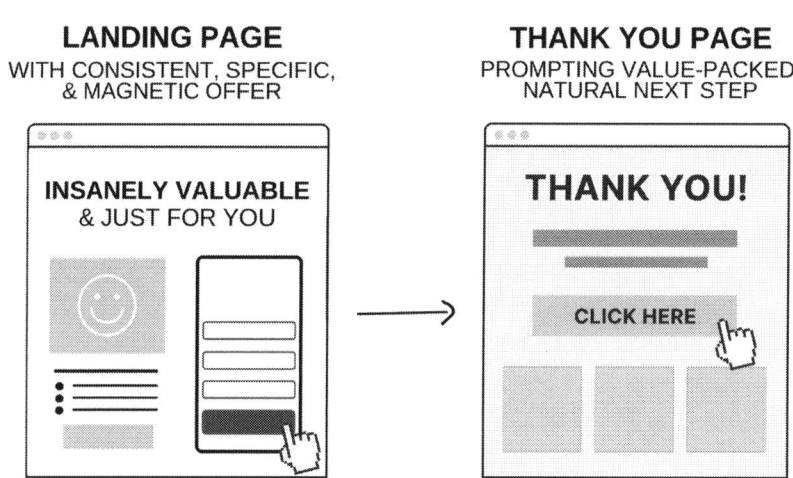

At the top of this page, you want to provide confirmation that whatever action they took on the first landing page was successful and that the ball is in motion.

Examples:

Thank you! Your xyz value-add is on the way.

Thank you! Your registration for the event has been confirmed.

Per usual, the next step on the thank you page will depend on the lead magnet.

If it's a top of funnel lead magnet for those who are new to your audience, this Thank You Page could be used to:

- ✓ Opt-in to your email newsletter
- ✓ Learn more about you on your website
- ✓ Check you out on social media
- ✓ Download another lead magnet
- ✓ Invite them to an event

Chapter 8

Basically, the Gym Isn't the Only Place Where #Gains Happen

Once you learn the rules of the game, you can start experimenting with and testing your own lead magnets and landing pages.

But all in all, the ONLY clickable action your landing page should offer is your CTA button—and the form attached to it—if it's relevant. That button or form along with compelling copy, headline, and images should all be above the fold, which basically means at the top.

Gaining new prospects and clients is inevitable by leveraging lead magnets and landing pages that are less about you, and more about what your prospect can gain.

And when your ideal audience **gains** value from your content and you can **gain** more prospects in your funnel—everybody wins.

Next Steps & Resources You Can Use *Today*

For a breakdown of the Four Main Types of Landing Pages (and where they might make sense in your funnels) download it here: www.truthaboutdm.com/landingpages

We broke down a few examples of lead magnets, but if you want more, don't miss this cheatsheet outlining 37 additional opportunities at: www.truthaboutdm.com/gain37

Chapter 9

How to Nurture Your List

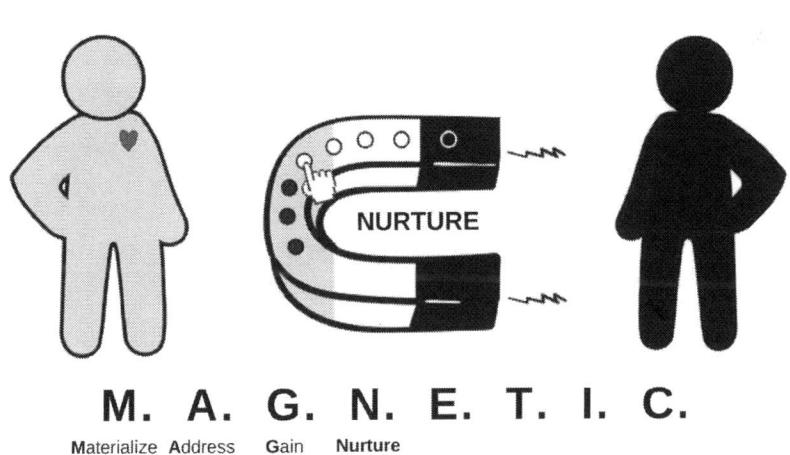

M. A. G. N. E. T. I. C.
Materialize Address Gain **Nurture**

The root of every hour spent online is dopamine, specifically a "dopamine-driven feedback loop".

Dopamine is a chemical released in your brain that signals pleasure and rewards you when you engage in enjoyable activities.

When you have a good meal, spend a sunny day outside, or get a good workout in, your brain releases dopamine.

What's interesting is that, not only is dopamine a part of your brain's reward system, but the processes that drive you to take action.

It makes you feel good, and it makes you want to do it again.

The Internet and/or your cell phone *alone* are not addictive. What makes us panic when we lose our phones and check our inboxes 20 times a day comes from how companies leverage the tools on our devices (likes, comments, news articles) to make us crave new stimuli.

This repeated cycle of activity, rewards, and being flooded with dopamine physically rewires our brains. Dopamine is one of the same chemicals involved when there's a drug addiction.

It's part of our natural biological system for survival. When your dopamine levels are low, you can suffer from sleep problems, fatigue, mood swings, memory loss, and more.

We'll take the quick hits of dopamine when we find an activity, like getting online, that will provide it.

We just can't get enough.

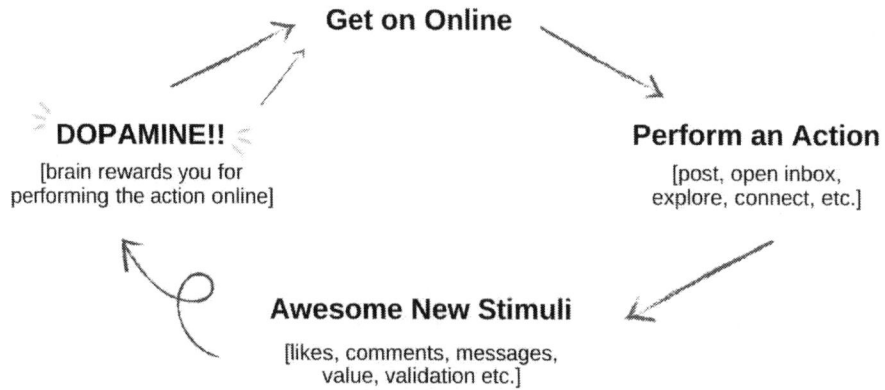

Chapter 9

Because a dopamine rush can also be triggered by successful social interactions and unexpected surprises, we can point to AOL's famous *"You've Got Mail!"* alert as the first digital dopamine delivery.

Today, if we heard that same, *"You've Got Mail!"* every time we got an email, I think we'd all go nuts.

Today? We get A LOT of emails. And texts. And digital messages.

Do we read and respond to all of them? Absolutely not.

Instead, when we pull up a browser or open our inbox, our brain is trained to look for the messages that are most likely to deliver the biggest amount of dopamine.

In any other setting, I'd tell you that I'm *not* a fan of the digital, dopamine-driven feedback loop. There's a reason why Steve Jobs wasn't on social media—along with many brilliant people inside (and outside of) the tech world. Consider this a fair warning for your personal life and mental health. This quick commentary may be counter-productive to the message of this whole book (LOL), but it is what it is. And I care about you guys.

If you're one of the few that is completely of the grid, you are my hero. Legit.

But…You're in the minority.

The addiction our audience has to their smart phones and inboxes is part of the gig. A key to capturing attention online and being the best online.

You and your content need to deliver the dopamine that your audience craves. Otherwise, people simply won't pay attention and will keep scrolling their inbox, their timeline, or whatever feed they're on until they find it.

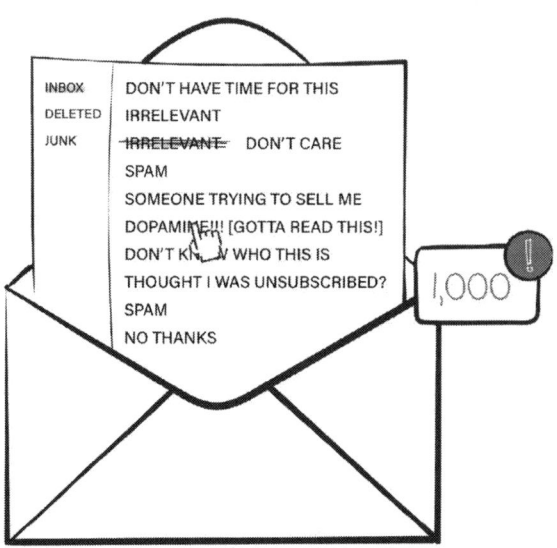

If you want to send emails that will get opened, read, and deepen your relationships with your audience, they should signal to your audience's subconscious that your communications are dopamine-rich.

Which, at the end of the day, is a pretty exciting opportunity and worthy endeavor. Creating a strategy to nurture your list that's dopamine-rich *simply means making them enjoyable.*

Advisors have an uphill battle here, just because they're advisors. Another place where many of the industry marketing companies haven't set advisors up for success.

But you *can* make your messages to your audience dopamine-rich. You *can* make people feel good about getting online, hearing from you, and want to hear more.

And you *should* be dialed-the-heck-in on nurturing your audience with enjoyable communications if you want to turn strangers on the internet into real-life clients.

1. Truth Is...**Getting into your audience's inbox = Getting into their heads (and hearts).**

You have a significantly better chance of reaching your audience via an email or text than you do reaching them by posting on a social media platform.

Every time you gather a new phone number or email address, you grow your pipeline and safeguard your practice against somehow losing access to your audience on social media.

On social media, even if customers and prospects like or follow your page, there is an infinitely complex algorithm that decides what gets delivered and what doesn't. You cannot reliably count on social media to serve every message that you share.

> As social media platforms move in and out of favor and algorithms change, you want to own your audience.

Day in and day out, one of your biggest focuses is to build your contact list, email list, text list, leads list.

Treasure your lists and treat them with care.

They are your direct line to your audience.

With emails, three things can happen (versus the 50 that can happen on social):

- It fits the email hosting's criteria for spam, or it doesn't
- It either hits their inbox, or it doesn't
- They read it, or they don't

For text? It delivers, they read it, and whatever happens next is up for grabs.

Building, respecting, and nurturing your lists means crafting communications that hit their inbox, get read, and add value, a.k.a., it doesn't go into their spam folder or is ignored alongside the alert for new clearance items at Dick's Sporting Goods.

I won't lie. Every day, it gets harder to hit someone's email inbox (or at least the one they regularly check).

A primary way email hosting companies like Gmail, Outlook, or Yahoo compete with one another, and protect current and future revenue, is by protecting your audiences' inboxes. Their battle is to be the email server that delivers the most dopamine.

Dopamine isn't delivered when someone receives a complicated, generic email about the economy.

You think the email hosting platforms see delivering a canned message as a competitive advantage? *Absolutely not.*

And they know when you are sending the same email as a thousand other people.

Think of the email hosts as the bouncer.

This is how they add value: Serving what seems to be valuable and relevant, and shielding their customers' attention from the rest.

If you've purchased a boilerplate drip campaign, there's a good chance it's not even hitting your lists inbox.

 FRIENDLY FYI: Going back to last chapter's conversation about lead magnets, the same thing applies. If you're using the same lead magnet with the same copy to introduce it, your rankings on

Google will suffer. Google also knows when you're using the same content as a hundred other advisors.

You cannot provide the empathy, transparency, and authenticity that propels our industry's elite advisors without giving your digital communications some TLC.

Having direct access to someone's inbox email or text inbox, is a major responsibility that should be treated with respect (and a little dopamine).

2. Truth Is...Who cares if the emails are automated if they're boring and irrelevant?

There is no reason why you or your team should wake up in the morning with no idea when you'll communicate with your audience next.

Automations are your friend. But there is a distinct difference between automations *for the sake of automating* and creating *intentional* automations that reinforce trust and rapport with your clients.

On one of our recent mastermind calls, an advisor out of Nashville said:

> "Automations create efficiency.
> They do not replace intimacy."

Your clients and prospects are smart enough to look at your emails, your text messages, your posts, and say, "This is automated," a.k.a., *"This was not crafted straight from this advisor's mouth. It does not come from the heart. I don't even know what this is. So, even if this person is 'talking' to me, why should I listen?"*

If you are still on the fence, and not quite ready to let go of using a third-party's marketing service, then *at the very least* sit down, in advance, and customize the messages so they better fit your brand, your voice, and what you know your ideal audience will best respond to.

The goal is to have automations that people *can't tell* are automations.

Automation is simply taking anything that can be done by a human and having it automated in a way that feels like real life.

Meaningful social interactions play a big role in delivering dopamine.

Go back though the last few emails you sent out to your list. Do they feel like personalized attempts at meaningful social interactions?

Remember, people do business with people.

You get what you give. **And if you're swiping your card for something you can set and forget, you're probably not really adding a whole lot of value to your clients.**

While email drip sequences are probably the easiest to purchase from a marketing vendor, they also tend to be the most canned.

Do you make the big bucks to write emails all day or redo the work that's already done and supposedly "proven?" Nope.

Can you create automated workflows *without* relying on third-party marketing companies? YES.

That's the value of having a team you can leverage.

Find someone to add to your team who can take this task off your plate without compromising your firm's personal touch.

Having a dedicated person to help you create and customize your content in advance will not only allow you to make sure all your messages are compliance-approved in advance, but it will create better results with prospects and better serve your *existing* clients in massive ways, too.

When Automation Works

Some communications need to be automated so it hits the prospect's inbox quickly, which helps with the trust factor.

Let's say your lead magnet is a compilation of show notes from all your best podcast episodes and a lead has just given you their information to download it.

That email better hit their inbox immediately.

And the automated communications shouldn't end with the delivery of your lead magnet. This is where a drip campaign comes in. A drip campaign or drip sequence is simply the automation of several communications over a period of time.

In this example, the first part of the drip sequence would be an email that says something like, *"Hi! Here are those resources you requested. Make sure you don't miss page three, which answers the number one question we get from people just like you."*

But this is where the real value in having a drip system comes in.

Yes, you've quickly delivered the value you promised, but that should only be the beginning. Now that you've gained access to their inbox, the door has opened for more direct opportunities to nurture your audience, create trust, and motivate them to take the next step.

This is also probably a great time to reiterate that your lead magnets *better be valuable.* If you send some fluff piece to get their contact information, they're not going to be super stoked to receive any future communications from you.

People will unsubscribe from your emails, or even worse, report you as spam, which compromises your ability to show up in your audience's inboxes in the future (and in some cases, will get you blocked from being able to send ANY marketing correspondences ever again!).

So, in our drip system, we have the lead magnet and something to deliver it, plan automated future communications to nurture the relationship and continue the conversation.

When you're talking about 25 different problems and have 25 separate lead magnets and inconsistent offers to enter your funnel…Creating a succinct, story-based email campaign that leads the audience down one specific path can be a daunting task.

You probably don't have the time to build 25 separate email automations that talk about every single problem you can help solve, nor do I think it's necessary to have in the first place.

When you're zoned in on exactly who you are, who you help, and have packaged your value proposition, email sequences will become significantly easier to craft and your efforts become much more streamlined.

Why? Because there's also consistency amongst your lead magnets—a.k.a. how people opt-in to your communications.

Several individual lead magnets could lead into the same core email sequence with a few small tweaks to reflect the specific lead magnet. No need to reinvent the wheel.

I could write a whole book about different email strategies, and who knows, maybe I will one day. For now, here are two of the most important and essential emails for any email nurturing strategy.

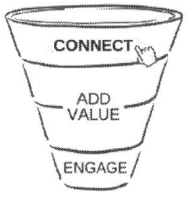 **[CONNECT] The Welcome Email**

The welcome email is the first email that goes out when someone joins your audience. Remember CAVE? Make sure you *connect* in that first email.

Look at your email sequences as an opportunity to take your prospects on a journey supported by a storyline. And the welcome email is the first chapter.

According to a study conducted in February 2021:

- The average open rate for a welcome email is 50 percent. That makes it 86 percent more effective than standard newsletters
- 76 percent of people *expect* to receive a welcome email immediately after subscribing to your list

- Users who receive a welcome email show 33 percent *more engagement* with the brand
- Welcome emails on average generate up to 320 percent *more revenue per email* than other promotional emails

When we consider the data, the welcome email is arguably the most important email you can send.

While your audience is at their peak interest, you'll want to make a strong first impression and tell the subconscious brain by delivering dopamine that it wants to not only receive, but read, your emails in the future.

Share some of your "why" and create an emotional connection while concisely reiterating what your firm does, for who, and how.

Train your email audience what to expect from you in future emails and prove to your recipients that your emails will not be a waste of their time.

Include directions on other ways to connect with you, address or reiterate a paint point, and provide a specific value-add that is above and beyond what they already signed up for.

 **[ENGAGE] The Nine-Word Email**

The shortest emails are the ones that get people to raise their hand and respond. Allow me to introduce my all-time favorite type of email: The Nine-Word Email.

Nine-word emails are not designed to share information, but to create engagement by asking a question to your email audience. It doesn't literally have to be nine words, but the shorter the better.

It might look something like this:

Name,

Just curious - do you know where your income will come from in retirement?

Name

One advisor I know and have worked with, Reno, said, "The nine-word email is the one that they're going to reply to 100 percent of the time. Not 100 percent of the people will reply to that, but whenever I get a reply, 9 times out of 10, it's from one of those emails."

He has several nine-word emails sprinkled throughout every email sequence he has.

3. Truth Is...**There's no point in getting past the bouncer if your friends inside can't find you.**

Sweet! So, your email clears the spam filters and lands in their primary inbox. Here's how you make sure it gets read.

Send your emails from a personal account

Go look at your email inbox. How many of them are from companies? And how many of them do you plan on opening, reading, engaging with? Of the emails that you have opened, again, how many of them came from a business versus an individual?

Most advisors who see results online will create a personal email address for marketing that is separate from the one they use to conduct business.

Send your emails from an account attached to a person's name, every time.

Personalize and make people feel special

Unlike a headline or a call to action, you can personalize your email subject lines to include the recipient's name, company, location, etc. This personalization will always catch the attention of people in their email inbox.

For example, you might say: *"(Name), are you free next Tuesday?"*

Even saying "you" and talking directly to your reader will improve your open rates. So, *"Are you free next Tuesday?"* can work.

Send your emails at the right times

To ensure your emails are at the top of someone's inbox, you want to make sure you're sending them when people are most likely to check email.

The "right time" is going to vary depending on your audience. Some people check their email when they first wake up, others wait to check their email until they're at the office. Some will check their emails late into the evening and on the weekends, and others only check their email when they're in front of their computer at work. The best time to send an email is going to be an individualized thing.

Artificial Intelligence can make it easier for you to send emails when the individuals in your audience are most likely to read them.

If you don't have an AI-based email marketing CRM, start with these general rules of thumb, and test it, just like anything else:

6 am—Sending first thing in the AM makes sense, because 50 percent of people start their day by checking their email.

10 am—This allows you to capture the attention of the person who may have had a busy morning or doesn't like to check their email until they're situated.

2 pm—Towards the end of the day and after lunch, there's going to be a group of your audience that is looking for a distraction or thinking about things other than work.

8-10 pm—Capture the attention of the people who check their email before bed.

 HACK FOR SCHEDULING EMAILS: If your emails are automated, try to schedule them so that they don't hit RIGHT on the hour, or at the same time every single day or week. If you're not strategic about how you set up your automated emails, you may indicate to the email host that the junk folder is the best place for your emails to go.

Friendly Copywriting Reminders

Every concept discussed in Chapter 7 about copywriting should translate to how your emails are composed. But there are three big ones to emphasize here.

YOUR AUDIENCE IS NOT GOING TO BE "HYPED" ABOUT "READING" EMAILS LIKE THESE.

Get your subject lines right

Your email subject line is just like your headline. It has to be compelling and attention grabbing—otherwise, your email simply won't get read.

Just like a good headline or call to action, you must persuade readers by answering the question: *Why should they read your email?*

What's in it for them if they read it? What can they expect to get out of it?

The shorter the better. People decide what emails they're going to read by scanning their inbox and opening what they perceive to be the most important and valuable.

Scanning is the key word.

Provoke readers to take action

Since your subject line is comparable to a CTA, using action-oriented language that creates urgency will help you not only get your email read, but encourages readers to take the action you want them to take inside of the email.

Don't talk AT people, talk WITH people

As you compete with everything else in your audience's inbox, remember that you set yourself up for failure if you ask or expect them to read emails with long, dense paragraphs or complex language. Lean into bullet points and a scannable format to ensure that your emails are easy to read.

If your emails are not concise and conversational, all it takes is one open for someone to decide your emails are too much work or irrelevant

Use the P.S.!

The most read part of an email is usually the P.S. at the end. Use that for your CTAs. A couple examples:

P.S. Want to learn more about the three key areas of retirement planning? Click HERE to visit our website.

P.S. Want to sit down with me, enjoy a fine meal (on us!) and get the whole rundown on our (xyz)? Click HERE to RSVP for a *Insert Firm Name / Event*.

P.S. Have you filed for Social Security yet? If not, please make sure you avoid making THIS mistake. Click HERE if you want to take 15 minutes to make sure you're not (xyz).

4. Truth Is...I can't NOT talk about texting.

Going deep on email was a no-brainer for three reasons:

1. The technology is easier to use—for both your team and your audience
2. It's more compliance-friendly
3. More people have an email address than texting capabilities

But, at a whopping 98 percent open rate, it is the most intimate and powerful inbox of all—especially for your bottom of funnel efforts.

For those of you who can't text, you're lucky my editor told me my book was too long and I should scrap this part. For those of you who can text or want to explore it, check out the *Truth Is: Texting Guide* at the end of this chapter.

You're going to want to use every opportunity to **nurture** your audience and online relationships—whether it's with email and/or text—you possibly can. And your nurturing strategy should be dopamine-rich and highly personalized at every single touchpoint.

Chapter 9

Next Steps & Resources You Can Use *Today*

To access an email case study highlighting specific tactics to create more impact and improve the copywriting in your nurturing strategy, head to: www.truthaboutdm.com/email

Love the idea of texting? Same. Your compliance good with it? Even better. Grab the *Truth Is: Guide to Texting* at: www.truthaboutdm.com/texting

Chapter 10

Elevating Your Impact with Videos

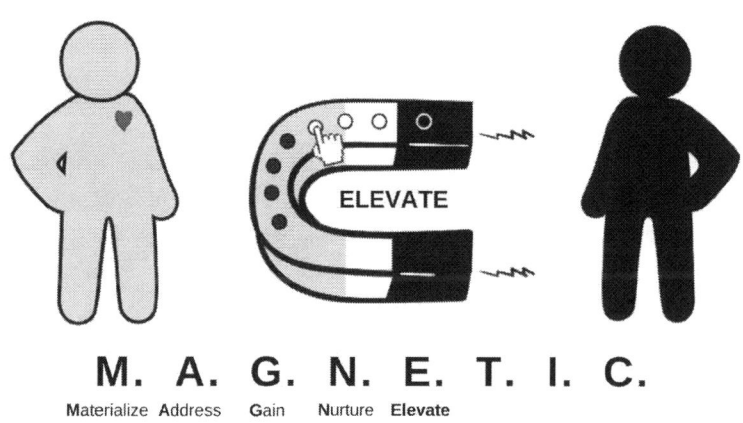

If a picture is worth a thousand words, how many words is a video worth?

One of the biggest opportunities for your firm is getting comfortable with videos, building systems to support them, and using them as much as possible.

When you're gathering and nurturing leads, videos **elevate** your entire digital strategy.

There's a reason why most of the content on the Internet is video. And that's not just because people don't really read stuff online.

Videos elevate:

- ✓ The connection with the viewer
- ✓ Their understanding (and retention) of your messages
- ✓ Your ability to engage the audience

I highly doubt I'm the first person to encourage you to use video in your digital marketing. And there's no way I'll be the last. My question to you is: How many of the people telling you to do video are really teaching you how to build that muscle?

Don't get me wrong. You will need to do your part, a.k.a. putting in the reps.

But I'm willing to bet that, again, our industry isn't doing a good enough job having on-camera coaching and behind-camera strategy readily available in the same way that canned videos are.

This chapter is for every advisor who is tired of being told to "do videos" but hasn't really had anyone break it down for them.

…Every advisor who tried a couple videos, didn't think it made a difference or that they were good on camera, and jumped ship.

…The advisors who are already crushing it on video and want to elevate their game.

…Those who have a bunch of videos and have no idea what to do with them.

This is for you.

You're going to walk away from this chapter with:

Chapter 10

1. A framework for how videos fit into a comprehensive funnel using The CAVE Conversion Formula™
2. Hacks for creating videos that both capture and keep attention
3. What to NOT do in your videos
4. What your necessary next steps are when the camera stops rolling

1. Truth Is...**Not all videos are created equal.**

There are several places you should use videos in your funnel. Let's look back at AIDA and CAVE.

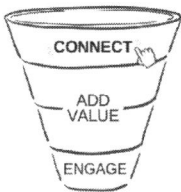
[CONNECT] Top of Funnel Videos

In your top of funnel content, videos should connect you to your prospect via an introduction about who you are and what you're about, create curiosity, and gently invite prospects to pay attention and engage further.

As an advisor, remember the hurdles your audience will clear and how those hurdles build as your audience progresses through your funnel. Remember: Time, Information, Anonymity.

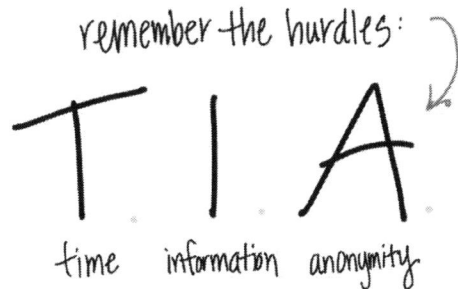

At the top of your funnel, especially before there's a connection, they won't be prepared to spend too much time with you, give you a whole lot of information, or put themselves in a situation where they have to talk to someone they're not ready to talk to.

In your top of funnel videos:

- → Keep the video between 30 to 60 seconds max
- → Don't ask viewers for contact information or to make any big commitments
- → Introduce yourself by highlighting who you are, what you stand for, the value of your team, and why you're worth paying attention to

Even in your top of funnel videos where you're simply laying the foundation for a relationship and future hurdles, use a CTA. When you use CTAs consistently throughout your funnel, you train your audience to expect them, get a chance to find out what resonates, and prime them for stronger CTAs in the future.

Sample messages for CTAs in top of funnel videos:

"Tell me about your experience in the comments."

"Stay until the end of the video for this one thing."

"Make sure you write this down."

Chapter 10

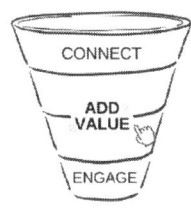

[ADD VALUE] Middle of Funnel Videos:

You already know what happens in your middle of the funnel videos. You're adding value. You'll also want to remind them who you are and reinforce the connection you've already established in your top of funnel videos.

Middle of funnel videos should:

- → Retarget your audience (hit the same people who saw your top of funnel video or already have an awareness of who you are and how you help people just like them)
- → Add value related to what you'll ultimately offer in a tone that communicates your intention to *serve*, not sell. This is about creating an interest and a desire more than it is about them taking action
- → Be 60 to 90 seconds max

The goal is that you've created enough of a connection and added enough value that you can use a stronger CTA to prompt your audience to take a next step towards engagement that is a bit more meaningful, but not a HARD CTA.

Sample messages for CTAs in middle of funnel videos:

"If this sounds like you, be sure to check out this thing."

"Avoid making the same mistake. Take this step to access this quick and simple resource that covers the three other things that can help you avoid it."

"One day, this is a decision you'll need to make. Follow this page or drop your info here for more."

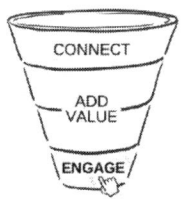

[ENGAGE] Bottom of Funnel Videos:

If someone is seeing a bottom of funnel video, they've cleared the lower hurdles and are potentially ready to take a bigger leap towards engagement. There's connection. Hopefully, because you've added massive value without telling them to book an appointment in every encounter just like every other advisor, you've created trust, credibility, autonomy, and potentially a sense of reciprocity for your viewer.

Consider the following for your bottom of funnel videos:

- → You can hit up to three minutes on this video, although I strongly recommend keeping it at or under two minutes
- → Don't wait until the very end of the video to provide that CTA. Hint at it at the beginning of your vid and nudge them to stick around so they don't miss it (and what they'll gain from it)
- → Always add additional value, or remind them of value they've already received, in your prompts to engage
- → Don't assume people will watch the whole video and use the text/platform where the video is being shared to reiterate the message and CTA

The viewer should feel like your relationship has more intimacy here, not less. Your relatability and the sense of hearing from a trusted, approachable source should be at its peak.

As much as you may feel inclined to go into sales mode and use your "phone voice" (I know you have one) when you're getting ready to drop that CTA, *don't*.

Otherwise, you'll potentially compromise the trust you've built thus far and jeopardize their willingness to commit to go further.

Resist the urge to SELL your CTA in your nonverbal communication on camera. Remember, they need your help.

Less is always more. The next step is no big deal and an absolute no brainer.

Sample Messages for CTAs in Bottom of Funnel Videos:

"If you aren't sure about which option is best in this case, text me at this number and we'll find 15 minutes to get your question answered."

"We've worked with X amount of people just like you. You can't do this thing without knowing this. Send an email here with the subject line "XYZ", your exact question, and why it matters."

"You can either spend hours sorting through what's on the Internet or what your friends say and unwinding it in the future. Or you can take 10 minutes today to (hopefully) gain clarity. Click the link directly below this video, find 10 minutes that work for you, and whether it makes sense to go further on this together or not, we'll make sure you get what you need."

2. Truth Is...**Most advisors make boring videos. People don't watch boring videos.**

I want our industry to stop creating videos based on what it thinks a video from a financial advisor should look like.

Take some time and look at some of the best video creators on the Internet outside of our industry. If you pull up Facebook or YouTube, you'll notice that pros don't record videos in a rigid office with a boring bookshelf behind them.

Nobody goes on social media to watch people talk at their desks about what—for most people—are the most boring and complex topics on the plane. Aside from simplifying your messaging, here's how to increase viewership, keep attention, and liven up those videos.

Get Comfy (and Real)

Get out of your suit, get out from behind your desk, and remember why people go on social media. Wear your Hawaiian shirt if it's your favorite. Record the video on your patio if that's your happy place. One, it'll help you be more comfortable and two, this shift will immediately translate to better videos.

Create Movement Through Pattern Disruptions

Did you know that, on average, TV shows and commercials change the scene every 10 seconds?

Experts refer to this technique as "pattern disruptions." Top YouTubers have taken this technique to the next level and on average use interrupt patterns every two seconds.

If you want to get attention, disrupt! Don't record videos of any length that are "static" (ie. Being a monotone bump on a log).

Other techniques you can use to disrupt the pattern and deliver the dopamine:
- Use images and graphics that reinforce the message on the screen
- Walk around, move your hands, create as much movement—without being distracting —as possible
- Modulate your expressions and tone—change your tempo, your facial expressions, your mood—to accomplish the same thing

Use Jump Cuts

One of the best pieces of advice I ever got on my video content was using an editing style called "jump cuts." It's a style that is very popular on YouTube that translates phenomenally on videos across all platforms.

It's basically slicing out the parts of your video that have long pauses or gaps so that your video flows from statement to statement. It's almost like you're interrupting yourself.

First, subconsciously, it makes you look like a super fancy content creator, even though anyone with a free app on their smartphone can do it (lol, like me).

But the real benefit is this: When the video "jumps," your brain receives the same stimuli and rush of dopamine that we've become so addicted to on social media because it is interpreted as another stimuli.

It feeds your brain's addiction to new, constant stimuli without prospects scrolling past your stuff to get it.

Think Long-Term

This isn't just about capturing attention in your first 10 videos.

This is about keeping attention for the next 100 videos.

If your videos all look the same, your audience will become fatigued by your content. The brain becomes desensitized to the same visual stimuli over and over and one will subconsciously think: *"I've seen a couple; I've seen them all."*

Shoot your videos from different angles and in different settings. Do one inside, and the next outside. Do them in different rooms. Remember, you want to create an audience for a lifetime.

3. Truth Is...**Creating great videos isn't as hard as you think.**

If you've ever watched a video and thought to yourself, "There's no way I can do that," give yourself a break.

My generation (sup millennials) is really the first to grow up talking to a camera or a screen. For us, it's natural. For each generation after us, it will become even more second nature. Which reinforces the fact that producing video content is something you need to get comfortable with if you want to stay relevant.

I get it, though. If you've never done it before, I know its intimidating. If I still had access to the first videos I recorded for video emails, you would laugh. They are hilarious. And, assuming you have a sense of humor, I'm sure your first stabs at video were probably a little funny as well. Here are a few ways to get over your nerves.

Don't try to be perfect

If you think you're going to be terrible on camera, you probably will be. Mindset is everything. I want to empower you to tell yourself that you can kick-ass on video because guess what, you can.

It may take practice, just like anything else. Put the reps in, embrace the inevitable discomfort that comes with meaningful growth, and go for it.

> You have more to lose by NOT using video than putting out a video that isn't perfect.

With every day that passes that your marketing strategy doesn't include videos, you're leaving opportunities on the table.

Don't read from a teleprompter

YES to video content. NO to reading from scripts or a teleprompter.

It's like—is this *really* how you feel? Are you speaking from the heart? Who wrote this script? Is this even your message?

In actual conversations, people blink, they say "um," they stumble over their words, they have run-on sentences, they smile, they do human things.

I'll watch a video where all those things are happening over a video with a robotic message delivery any day of the week. So will your audience.

Here's what you do instead:

Use an outline in advance, know the talking points, and roll with it. If you must memorize any part of the video, it needs to be your first sentence and the call to action. The value in between should flow naturally if you know the bullet points since this is your area of expertise.

Will those videos be perfect? NOPE. But they'll be a massive improvement.

And honestly: No video is ever perfect. There is not a single video I have ever created or posted that I've been like "YUP!!! Wouldn't change a single thing about this."

That's what it means to be a creator.

Video scripts are a lot like copywriting

Any of the copywriting formulas included in Chapter 7, or the free download of 37 copywriting formulas, also serve as video scripts. I'll add that download again at the end of this chapter.

Do I want you reading from a script? Absolutely nor. But writing scripts is helpful. Obviously, they help with compliance approval, but they also help you avoid recording videos you expect to last for 45 seconds but go on for four whole minutes.

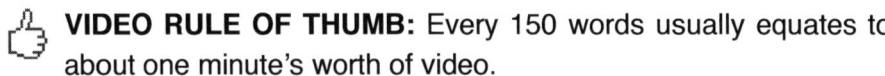 **VIDEO RULE OF THUMB:** Every 150 words usually equates to about one minute's worth of video.

You need to capture attention before you can keep it. So, in the same way that your headline is the most important piece of your copywriting, the opening to your video should give your audience dopamine whiplash. Like, "*WHAT?*"

Chapter 10

You have eight seconds to get their attention. Bring the climax of your videos to the very beginning.

Let's pretend you're recording a video about the Titanic.

Sample Video Opening #1:

"A cruise ship split in half and sunk to the bottom of the ocean alongside hundreds of thousands of people, and these two soulmates STILL found each other among the pieces of ice in the water."

Sample Transition #1:

"There are a thousand reasons why that boat shouldn't have gone down, and here's the one that did…"

And then you rewind, tell the story that brings them to the climax, and drop the CTA.

Here's another example. If you know anything about me, you know that there's no way I'm publishing a book without talking about the Philadelphia Eagles. This one goes out for our Super Bowl win against the Patriots as the underdogs.

Sample Video Opening #2:

"What are the odds of a backup quarterback who had only started two games beating the greatest QB of all time on the NFL's biggest stage? Slim to none. But…He did it."

Sample Transition #2:

"Here's how it happened…"

#GoBirds #ThoughtTomWasTheGOAT? :)

CTA'S IN VIDEOS: If it's a middle or bottom of funnel video, find a way in the transition to reference your benefit-oriented CTA sooner rather than later.

4. Truth Is...**You aren't done once the video is recorded.**

If your video is going to have legs, you can't just record and hit upload. You've got to follow all the way through and do some editing.

The two basic things you'll want to include and optimize for every video are subtitles and thumbnails.

Wanna Ensure People Get Your Message? Use Subtitles

Think about where you are and what you're doing when you're on social media or browsing online. You're standing in line, sitting in a virtual meeting, watching your kids' soccer practice, doing things in places where it's not ideal to have your device's audio blasting.

Unless you live with your headphones in your ear or you pop them in to watch videos on social media (highly unlikely), you're not using the audio (unless you don't care about annoying the people around you, and if so, lol hey man do your thing).

> When your videos don't have subtitles, you're limiting your reach.

Here's the deal:

- More than 2 in 3 people watch video with the sound off in public places
- 1 in 4 people watch video with the sound off in private places
- 4 in 5 people are more likely to watch an entire video when captions are available
- 1 in 2 consumers say captions are important because they prefer to watch video with sound off

Those are some BIG NUMBERS.

This essentially means that: For every 100 people who are exposed to your video, there are between 25 to 80 people who will miss the message if there aren't subtitles.

Use subtitles to increase your engagement—otherwise you're wasting your time.

People Judge the Video by its Thumbnail

Depending on where the video shows up and your audience's settings, videos may not play automatically. A couple great examples would be on your website, in a blog, in an email, on YouTube, and on social media.

In this scenario, you want to use the video's thumbnail to grab your audience's attention and entice them to click "play" and watch the video you worked so hard to create.

A thumbnail is a still image that acts as a preview. It's almost like an album cover.

Here's a great example from Nick on his YouTube Channel:

A good thumbnail not only makes you and your videos look more professional, but it also makes people want to watch the video.

90 percent of the top performing videos on YouTube use a custom thumbnail.

In absence of a thumbnail, the platform the video is being uploaded to will choose the thumbnail for you from one of the still images. Which, LOL, is not usually effective OR super flattering.

Have your graphic design person create a custom thumbnail for every video you create.

Again, I know videos can be uncomfortable if you aren't used to making them. It's a muscle you have to build.

But I want you to take the recommendations to do video seriously. You cannot compete in digital marketing without some kind of video presence. Smile, get real, and get excited about all the ways using video can help **elevate** your firm, your digital presence, and the outcomes for your clients.

If it helps, there's a guide in the resources section for other types of custom, engaging videos you can create without having to get in front of a camera. Honestly, probably doesn't hurt to check them out, even if you already are crushing it on camera. A lil' pattern disruption never hurts.

Next Steps & Resources You Can Use *Today*

Ever wondered where and when you should use a vertically-oriented video horizontal—and vice versa? Find out the strategic difference at: www.truthaboutdm.com/video

If you aren't ready to make your video debut, but you're open-minded to learning about alternative ways to create and share videos (without hopping on camera), learn about the loopholes at: www.truthaboutdm.com/loopholes

Just incase you missed it in Chapter 7, make sure you grab the copywriting formulas so you can create the same impact in video scripts: www.truthaboutdm.com/copywriting

Chapter 11

(Tailored) Content is King

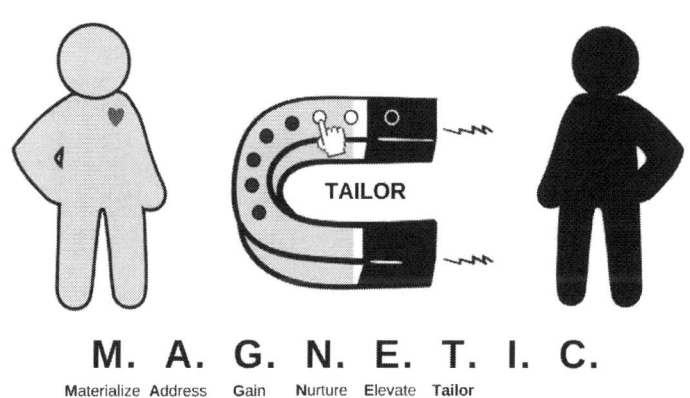

You've probably heard the phrase "content is king."

That isn't an idea that emerged in the last 10, or even 100, years.

Before there was digital, there was broadcasting.

Before broadcasting, it was print.

The origin of content marketing truly began over 1,000 years ago when Johannes Gutenberg invented the printing press in 1450.

This invention created the ability to spread information to larger audiences than previously possible through books, newspapers, and other printable mass communications.

As the technology for printed materials evolved, the printing press was inevitably used by entities to promote products and services. For example, Benjamin Franklin, a content marketing OG, printed and leveraged a book called *The Poor Man's Almanack* in 1732 to promote his own printing company.

Regardless of the technology or medium, the concept of content marketing, or using content to help sell products and services, can be seen throughout history.

One of the landmark campaigns in the evolution of content marketing is credited to John Deere, which in 1895 published an educational and content rich magazine for farmers called *The Furrow* to promote his company's farming products and services through adding value.

In 1933, Proctor and Gamble created a "radio soap opera" to promote their soap products.

In 1959, Exxon was one of the first to take a multi-platform approach to content marketing. Their "Put a Tiger in Your Tank" campaign was an early, prominent example of adapting and distributing across print, radio, and TV.

And now we have the Internet.

Regardless of the platform, where technology is today, and where it is going in the future, content is king.

So…Content *marketing* is non-negotiable.

The challenge is not only to simply understand what it means to create and deliver good content but also **tailoring** the content you serve based

Chapter 11

on the purpose, where it shows up, and how the digital landscape evolves.

In this chapter, we're going to:

1. Lay the foundation for your organic content
2. Dive into paid advertising
3. Talk about unmissable content categories
4. Break down how to use systems to become a robust, content making machine

1. Truth Is...**Organic content marketing is a long game worth playing.**

Organic content is any content that is not paid for. It's the free stuff that you upload, post, and share with your audience.

This includes:

- Any unpaid content shared on social media
- Blogs
- General lead magnets, videos, content on your website
- Emails
- Articles
- Public relations, ie. your website
- Your social media pages and presence
- Podcasts

Your organic content:

- ✓ Establishes your voice and presence
- ✓ Contributes to brand awareness
- ✓ Engages active members of your immediate audience
- ✓ Builds and nurtures relationships
- ✓ Supports paid marketing efforts

Many advisors try to skip the organic content and go straight to the paid content and campaigns to speed up results and viewership. Trust me, I get it. Every day I come up with a new idea that I wanted to do yesterday. And when I do get results, it's never fast or big enough. A lot of elite advisors operate the same way. It's exhausting LOL.

However…**You can't take shortcuts with your organic content and presence.**

Organic content should show up at every stage in your funnel. Some people say, and many believe, that organic content is only for your top of funnel content. It's not.

Use it to add value and engage your prospects. Leverage it to stay top of mind and engage with your clients as well. Not all of your results online will come from paid content and ads.

Be Patient!

Organic content marketing is a long game and you've got to be prepared to play all four quarters if you want to create true brand equity and maximize the effectiveness of your marketing spend on paid campaigns.

For reference, my prominence on LinkedIn via consistently showing up with fresh, organic content took about two or three years to establish. In my fourth year of consistently showing up, I was invited on tour with The Rolling Stones and The Alliance for Lifetime Income.

You reap what you sow.

An organic audience that has been built over time is *real*. It's *yours*.

> The attention you're capturing via a true organic presence is not because you've purchased or rented it—*you've earned it.*

Plus, it doesn't make sense to spend money on messages and offers without some gauge on whether they organically work.

This means creating the habits and processes to consistently show up long-term and identify what works for your team and your audience. In the meantime, you build a foundation of people who buy-in via earned engagement.

2. Truth Is...**Paid content buys more than just eyeballs. It keeps you in front of your audience** *all the time*.

Unlike organic content, where you basically must play the long game, stay consistent, and hope you get in front of the right people, paid advertising can immediately serve your content directly to your audience, wherever they are.

Your paid content:

- ✓ Expands the reach of your organic content
- ✓ Precisely targets audiences
- ✓ Delivers accelerated results

Advisors have a similar sentiment and approach to paid advertisements as they do organic content but flipped.

Just like organic content isn't just for the top of funnel, paid content is *not* only for bottom of funnel opportunities to book an appointment.

And your paid advertising campaigns will vary accordingly.

With that said, there are three massive benefits that paid content has over organic.

Paid Content Benefit #1: Instant Insights

At every incremental stage of a campaign, from the ads to the landing pages to the emails, you get instantaneous insights on what's working and what isn't. This real-time data allows you to make immediate adjustments to improve your results.

Paid Content Benefit #2: Laser-Focused Targeting

Using paid content campaigns creates the opportunity to get super specific in who you want your content served to.

Anything and everything from:

- ✓ Demographics
- ✓ Age—and specifically their generational cohort
- ✓ Gender
- ✓ Interests
- ✓ Location
- ✓ Brands they engage with
- ✓ Things they search
- ✓ Upcoming anniversaries
- ✓ Job changes
- ✓ How many people live in their household
- ✓ If they're in a new relationship
- ✓ People who travel, or have recently travelled
- ✓ Political views
- ✓ The type of phone or computer they use
- ✓ Their email hosting service
- ✓ Events they've attended

The list goes on. This is just the tip of the iceberg.

Because you're paying for it, you're guaranteeing it gets delivered. The more money you put behind a piece of content, the more people will see it.

Chapter 11

 MONEY'S NOT EVERYTHING: Just because you paid for it and your audience "sees" the content, doesn't mean the ads will work. It still needs to be attention-grabbing, valuable, and relevant if you want it to be money well spent.

There's an insane amount of information out there constantly being gathered. And if you want to win the game, you need to know the rules.

How can you leverage technology to gather data, maximize efforts, and increase your firm's equity? Know how to use "the pixel".

> Imagine if you could send out 40 different mail campaigns, and only have the mailers *with the highest RSVPs* hit the mailboxes?

Imagine a world where your mailers got smarter by leveraging insights like:

- ✓ How many mailboxes they have and which one they check the most
- ✓ How often they check their mail
- ✓ The type of mailbox
- ✓ What mail they read and what goes straight into the trash

- ✓ If they are more likely to read the mail on the top of the stack or the bottom

That's what "the pixel" does. The pixel is a tool used by paid advertising platforms to identify your ideal clients, follow them around online, and keep you in front of them.

It captures information about your audience's interests, preferences, and activity online and delivers your advertisements in the exact places and formats that they frequent and are likely to engage with.

Sound complicated? It's not. The pixel and the platforms that host them (ie. Facebook, Google, LinkedIn) do most of the work. You just need to drop the code onto the back of your website and landing pages.

With that said, putting the pixel on the back end of your sites doesn't do you any good if you sleep on it. Having a pixel is not the same as using one. Be sure to actively monitor and maximize the pixel's insights about your audience and campaigns by continuing to test new campaigns and markets.

Paid Content Benefit #3: Laser-Focused *Re-Targeting*

This is where it gets fun, and a little unsettling when you're on the receiving end of a good re-targeting campaign.

Part of having insights on what's working and what's not means leveraging that information to go back to the individuals who didn't convert initially and stay in front of them.

Have you ever visited a website and then had similar content and ads follow you around on the Internet?

It just happened to me the other day. I was on the Nike website looking for a new pair of shoes for CrossFit. By that afternoon, Nike ads for shoes showed up on my Facebook timeline and in ads on various web browsers.

I'll be honest: I am now the owner of a brand-new pair of Nike Metcons. They got me.

I know this has happened to you before. And, if you've ever had a marketing company talk about paid ads or following your audience around on the Internet, they're doing the same thing.

They're simply using the pixel to re-target your audience and continuously serve them content related to your event that they're most likely to engage with.

That's how Nike got me. And I'm HYPED about my new sneakers.

[USING A PIXEL FOR RETARGETTING]

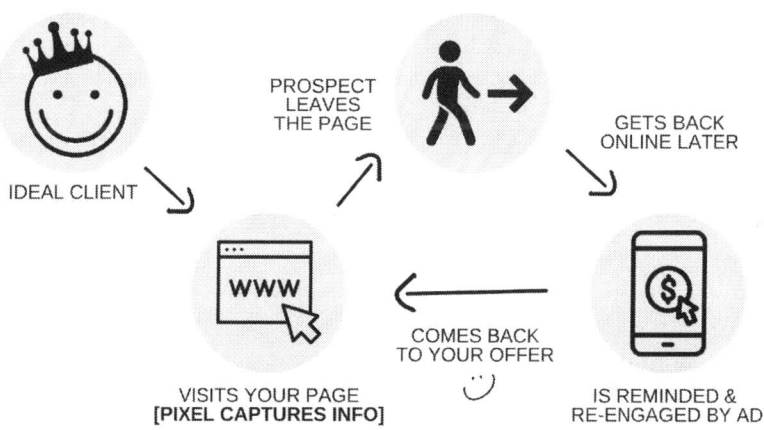

That's the power of the pixel and all its data.

Here's the best part: You're offering something way more valuable than comfortable and stylish (and overpriced) sneakers. As a financial advisor, you *change lives.*

If you can't beat 'em, join 'em.

Proceed with Caution

Are there clear benefits and advantages of running paid ads? YES. But it's not a magic potion. There are things you *have* to understand and consider before you dump a ton of money into an ad campaign.

Paid Content Truth #1: Having a Pixel Doesn't Guarantee your Ideal Outcome

Here's the big thing you need to know if you have anyone running outside ad campaigns for you: It's highly likely they're using a master pixel, not a custom one.

If a marketing company is running Facebook ads for you to fill an event, for example, chances are, they're not creating a custom pixel for your office and instead using a master pixel. Master pixels are not trained to go after the clients in your ideal audience. Instead, they target commonalities within your industry.

It would be as if Nike, Cole Haan, Crocs, and Louis Vuitton all used the same "master pixel" to collect data and run ads.

The data on the pixel gets watered down and ultimately will go after anyone who buys shoes.

Yes, the companies in the example all make and sell shoes, but the shoes, the people buying them, and the reasons why someone would wear those shoes are not interchangeable.

Just like you and your firm are not interchangeable with every single other firm using the same pixel.

Your brand equity matters.

If you're going to spend tens of thousands—and for some—hundreds of thousands of dollars, on paid advertising campaigns, you need to have more to show than just your results.

You need to have your own pixel.

When you stop using whoever has you on a master pixel, you have two choices:

Choice #1—Hop onto another (very smart, but equally generic) master pixel from another vendor

Choice #2—Create your own pixel, put it on the back of end of your digital campaigns and assets with the long-term goal of creating your own, highly intelligent pixel

If taking the leap away from a third-party marketing service is not feasible for you right now, no problem. Now you know. But if you are, you need to ask any vendor that is running any type of paid online campaigns for you to put your own custom pixel on the back of your website, blogs, and landing pages so it can start gathering information about who is visiting your site and eventually re-target them.

If they won't, find someone who will.

Paid Content Truth #2: Know When to Pull in an Expert

Most advisors running advertisements, or industry marketing companies running advertisements on their behalf, don't do enough testing to find out which audience, messaging, or content type will create the most conversations.

You would never tell a client to put all their eggs in one basket, so why would you pay someone to do that in their marketing?

Remember in Tom from Chapter 5? The digital marketing expert who blew every industry event funnel I've ever seen out of the water in 48 hours for our boy Cameron?

When true experts, including Tom, run ad campaigns, they do more testing on a single campaign than most amateurs might do over their entire career.

Slight exaggeration, but the testing is a BIG DEAL.

"When we studied the typical campaign of a financial advisor, and we went to their ads library, more often than not, there was only one advertisement or so running, and that was it. Whereas, what we'll do is sometimes launch 20 to 30 ads at a time with several variations of copy, headlines, call to actions, videos, pictures, or using different colors."
-Tom

The testing is crucial. Even for one of the world's most sought-after traffic companies rolling out 30 to 40 ads at a time, they'll find *70 to 80 percent of them won't work.*

It's a very essential, though tedious, way to find out which ones are the winners. So, even if the third-party running ads for hundreds of advisors uses an ad with specific copy or a specific format that has been tested in other markets, it doesn't mean they will work in yours.

With today's technology, experts can cross test different combinations of media, copy, and CTAs and have the winning combo automatically served to your audience.

I want to challenge you to think about the experts you work with and ask yourself: What makes this person an *expert*?

Are they an expert based on the quantity of advisors they work with or the quality of their results, research, and personalization?

Paid Content Truth #3: Ad Fatigue is No Joke

You know how you stop paying attention to the things you see all the time?

For example, when a commercial comes on TV that you've seen a thousand times, you change the channel or look at your phone until the commercial is over?

That's exactly what your audience will do if they are overexposed to the same content. They become bored and stop paying attention, which ultimately lowers the effectiveness of your marketing, makes your investment in paid ads less effective, and negatively affects your firm's bottom line.

This is known as *ad fatigue*. Any world class marketing machine that is putting money behind content knows that it's a requirement to actively mitigate ad fatigue by consistently pushing out fresh, high-quality content and undergoing the ongoing testing referenced earlier.

Ad fatigue is avoidable.

Unfortunately, many of the vendors inside the industry do not have the capacity or infrastructure to support the necessary testing and rejuvenation to support an effective paid content strategy over the long-term.

When you evaluate the specialist running your paid traffic, make sure you ask them to prove their commitment to ongoing testing and new content before you hire them.

3. Truth Is...**You will not see results if you only post about business.**

Have you ever been to a party where you get stuck with someone who seems incapable of talking about something other than their business and all its foreign and complex technicalities when all you want to do is go join the game of jumbo Jenga by the cooler?

Of course, you have. Don't be that guy.

Unlike in real life, you can ignore whoever and whatever you want when you're on the Internet.

As much as we might wish sometimes that we could mute or exit out of real-life conversations with no consequences, it's not an option. Being able to do that online without hesitation, is a luxury.

> A lot of the financial planning content I see from advisors today is way more interesting to *them* than to their audience.

Let me make myself very clear: Your content, regardless of the platform or method of delivery, cannot be all about business.

 AMIRITE OR AMIRITE: A lot of the time, people who actively seek out social media accounts that talk about the super technical and more-than-knee-deep investing and financial planning concepts are hardcore DIYers. Not the best or easier prospect to convert, am I right?

A Winning Content Formula

The goal of your social media strategy is to consistently share unique, valuable content across a few key categories that create distinctly unique connection points. The way I see it, there are three main organic categories, which I like to refer to as PEP.

Personal: If you want your brand and services to *resonate* with people, use transparency and vulnerability in a way that creates empathy

Entertaining, Enlightening, and Educational: The Three Big E's. If you want people to *like* your brand, lean into opportunities to make people smile and feel good about themselves.

Professional: If you want people to *trust* you and one day *take that next step*, tell stories about the problems you can help people solve.

Personal

Your personal content attracts people to your social accounts and keeps them around long enough to see your business content and say, "Hmm...Well. I like this person. They seem a lot like me. And they share a lot of great stuff. I'll stick around to hear what they're offering."

This is you just being yourself. Sharing pictures of your adventures with your family and friends. Telling stories about your latest win and tapping into your audience when you want advice. The obligatory pictures of your child's first day at school (or if you're a pet parent like me — of your dog and a cake on its birthday).

Choosing a financial advisor is very different from hiring a carpet cleaner or mechanic to fix your car. If you're a financial advisor, you're in the relationship business.

The personal is VERY important. Especially for you.

People's money is one of the most intimate and sacred aspects of their life.

The exception is when that financial decision is highly specialized and there are only one or two people in the entire country who know how to solve it. Then, the personal stuff probably doesn't matter as much.

But I'm telling you, more often than not, it matters A LOT.

What makes you human? What are you interested in? What makes you excited (or not so excited) to get out of bed in the morning?

Getting personal is paramount.

It's your opportunity to attract and create trust on an emotional level.

Entertaining, Enlightening, and Educational

This is basically a catchall. People love this stuff! These are the videos of the dog that is singing along with their owner. The quotes that make you think. The stuff that you and like-minded people will find fascinating.

Don't think too much about what falls under this category. Does it inspire you? Did it make you laugh? Did you want to show your best friend? Send it in a group text? Great. Use that.

For example—I see a lot of marketing companies providing recipes. And recipes can make for great content! But, if you don't like or have the time to cook, don't post recipes.

This is a place where I say, screw the data. I know you know someone who will scroll past a recipe and has no interest in cooking. If you don't, now you do. I'm a "throw it in the air fryer or a blender and call it a day" type of gal.

Make sure you post things that matter to *you* rather than trying to appeal to the things that you think everyone likes. Focus on things that you and your ideal client have a shared interest in.

The content you post should be something you can start or have a conversation about in real life as a mutual point of interest.

If not, keep scrolling. Your ideal client will do the same.

Professional

Storytelling is always important, but especially in your professional content.

When we tell stories, especially stories that show you *care*, the message comes across as an effort to add value and educate— as opposed to "Hey, do this thing so I can make some money."

There's a huge difference between: *"Only 2 percent of people are prepared for retirement at this age"...*

And: *"You know, I once worked with a guy, and when he came to our team, he had been presented with this decision. And it was a tough one, right? Because, he had to consider this, this, and this...and eventually we took this action and it was awesome, because this is the outcome he avoided."*

In your seminars and real-life conversations, you already tell stories of all the Bobs you've helped over the years, so why wouldn't you make storytelling a major part of your content strategy?

Facts tell, stories sell.

As always, the professional content and CTAs will vary depending on whether your audience is cold or warm. Your audience will be a mixed bag—and the minority is ready to work with you—so alternate between various levels of hurdles to ensure you're meeting people where they are. Here's some examples:

Top of Funnel Professional Stories:

- → **Stories to Tell:** Who you are as a human being, what makes you credible, what you're known for/believe in, and what that means for the people you serve
- ✓ **Result:** An awareness of you and a problem you can help them solve or a life you can help them live

Middle of Funnel Professional Stories:

- → **Stories to Tell:** Problems solved or avoided, and outcomes created by people just like them and how they can achieve the same results
- ✓ **Result:** An interest or desire in letting you be the person to help them solve that same problem

End of Funnel Professional Stories:

→ **Stories to Tell:** More specific stories and case studies that illustrate how that person met you, how that first meeting went, what was important, what it looked like after becoming a client, and the transformation they experienced
✓ **Result:** Readiness to act and experience that same transformation

Nothing will serve you more than dialing back the pressure on booking an appointment in every post and instead, telling stories about how your business helps people be happier and live better lives.

Not even an article about tax law.

TELLING STORIES WITH SOCIAL PROOF: To learn exactly how one advisor's social media content strategy provides social proof to bring in new clients and a case study of his compliance-approved, testimonial workaround, head to: www.truthaboutdm.com/workaround.

4. Truth Is...The key to content is consistent creation.

When you think about content creation, the focus usually goes straight to the content, but the key word here is *creation*.

> When you create the content, you create an audience.

You gotta participate in the part where the content is created. With that said, I know, *consistent* content creation is one of the hardest things to do. As someone who has been creating fresh, weekly content for just *one* platform for the past seven years, I know it's difficult.

Here are a couple of frameworks that will change the way you think about content creation.

Document, Don't Create:

Dan Sullivan once said, "Procrastination is a form of wisdom." In other words, procrastination shows us what we don't want to do.

You wanna know what I drag my feet on as a content creator?

Creating content. Which often looks like sitting down, racking my brain for something "good," hurrying to throw it together, and hoping it doesn't completely bomb.

Can you relate?

Sitting down, thinking, brainstorming, writing, recording, creating content takes a TON of organization and discipline.

So, stop creating it. :)

Instead, just start DOCUMENTING everything you do. Think about all the *gold* you do, say, and share daily. How often you answer the same questions to prospects. The conversations you have internally about planning philosophies. The things you say in weekly meetings with your team. The messages at your educational events.

The best performing content is usually off the cuff, raw, and comes from the heart.

In other words, it's not forced. It's not content for the sake of content.

It's the stuff that just *spills* out of you.

For example, check out this gem from behavioral finance expert Daniel Crosby that went viral, and even got *Elon Musk's* attention, on Twitter.

How crazy is that!? LOL, as a NYT best-selling author, psychologist, and keynote industry speaker…The content that went viral was an off-the-cuff, sarcastic post about Diet Coke. Of all things.

Was this the most relevant tweet to Daniel and his career? Nope. But did it open doors for him professionally? At more than 30 million views…100 percent.

You already know he was contacted by industry publications for interviews about any potential takeaways from his experience going viral related to behavioral finance.

Now, is it efficient, predictable, and streamlined to just wait for ideas to hit you when you're in the shower and let it rip when the lightning strikes?

Nope. So, where's the balance?

Right here:

> If you can capture and document as much of what you say and do as possible, you can efficiently create bomb content without "creating" content.

Why would you sit down and rack your brain and try to craft a message when you can document it and have it at the tip of your fingers?

Set up a camera or use the audio recorder on your phone to document your meetings and conversations. Document your client presentations and conversations, too. Hire a videographer to spend a day in your office every month or record big events.

There's no reason to spend three hours creating content when you could spend two of those hours doing revenue generating activities, capturing the gold, spending 30 minutes outlining where there may be value, and passing it off to a teammate or freelancer to polish.

Repurpose what you already have:

Thinking like a CEO means looking for leverage.

Thinking like a CEO *who has a good grasp on digital marketing* means knowing that any piece of content can be leveraged and repurposed across several platforms.

There is not a single piece of content that you create that will serve just ONE purpose.

One office I work with that brings on more than $20 million a year through their robust content strategy will do the following for every single video:

→ Take the transcription and turn it into a blog post
→ Use that transcription and turn it into an email
→ Have the full video put on YouTube
→ Have the video chopped up into several smaller videos that can be used on social media, a website, or a landing page

One video or conversation can be used over and over again.

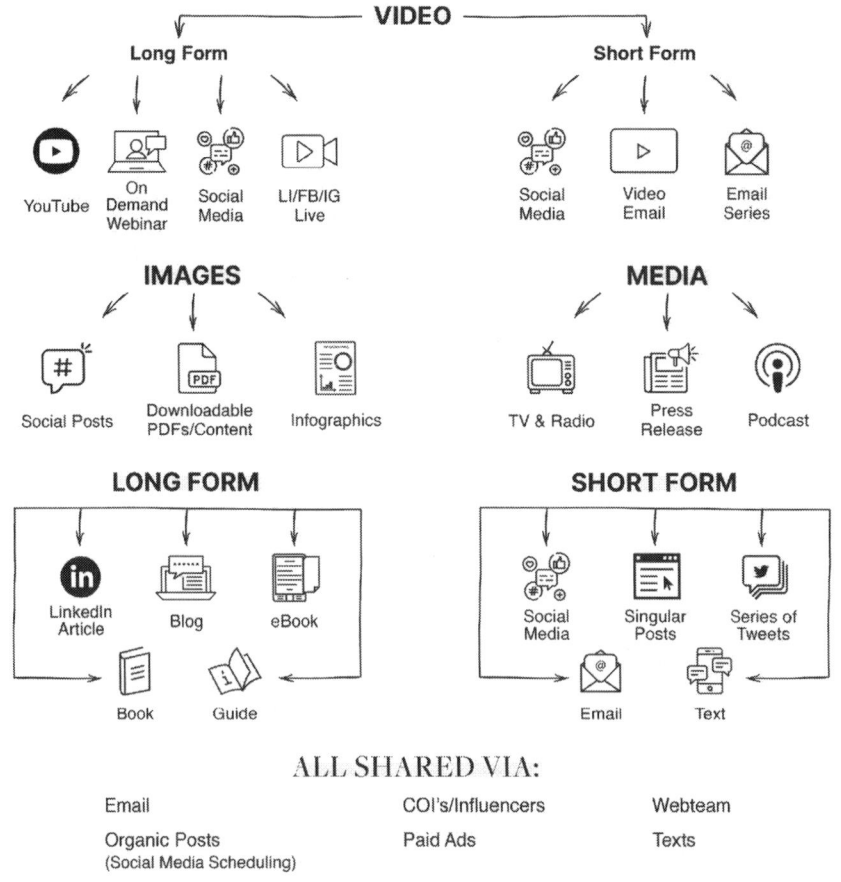

If someone doesn't watch that first video, but you have a way to serve it up three or four different ways, the time you spent creating that video goes significantly farther and you'll get new responses every single time.

Content creation, and then repurposing that content, should be one of yours and your firm's biggest priorities.

Content Curation:

A destination website (BuzzFeed, Barstool Sports) is a place where content is curated from all over the web with its audience in mind. That curated content may include original content directly from the source, but includes third party content from other brands, people. Its intent is to create a central source for the audience to get the content that they love to consume without sifting through everything on the internet.

Approach your online pages as a destination website for your audience. You'll still want to create your own original content, but here's why incorporating content curation makes sense.

Intentional content curation:

- ✓ Takes the pressure off you to create every single piece of content
- ✓ Is easy to delegate to a marketing team that understands what's meaningful to your audience
- ✓ Does not detract from your credibility, because you're still the source

The third point is a big one. Even if you're not the original voice sharing the message, you get bonus points with your audience for being the person who put the message in front of them (alongside your two cents about why your audience should pay attention to it).

Remember, There's No "I" in Scale:

To achieve true scale, your business cannot depend entirely on you.

Once you've hit the level of success where your calendar is stacked with first appointments plus client reviews, the next step for scale is bringing in someone who can take the service work off your desk.

Part of scale and specialization within your org chart includes having service advisors handle reviews for existing clients so you can focus on doing what you do best.

Bringing a service advisor on and successfully transitioning your clients with confidence to a new relationship is a process, and it must be done correctly if you want to maintain those relationships. This is hard to do when you're the only person they've seen in any of their marketing leading up to the relationship and the primary point of contact.

SUPER hard to do when your firm is named after you.

The roadmap to hiring and elevating other client-facing teammates is a topic for another day.

But your digital marketing should support your team approach. If you don't want to be the only person serving your new clients, you can't be the only person representing your company online.

Empower your team, show them off, and make documenting/repurposing gold from your *team* a part of the content strategy. *Especially* in your organic content, since it plays a major role in both brand awareness and client experience.

Remember, content is king. But, in the Attention Economy, it can't just be content for the sake of content. Create authentic and engaging content that's **tailored** to your ideal audience—no matter where they are in your funnel or how they prefer to consumer content.

Chapter 11

Next Steps & Resources You Can Use *Today*

For a quick download outlining the 25 different ways you can repurpose video content, download it at: www.truthaboutdm.com/25videos

Wanna see how I approach documenting (not creating) content to share my podcast interviews on social media? Watch the video tutorial: www.truthaboutdm.com/setup

Don't forget The 10-80-10 Rule. Use this worksheet to delegate and empower a teammate to own your content creation: www.truthaboutdm.com/content108010

To learn exactly how one advisor's social media content strategy provides social proof to bring in new clients and a case study of his compliance-approved, testimonial workaround, head to: www.truthaboutdm.com/workaround

Chapter 12

Social Media is an Investment

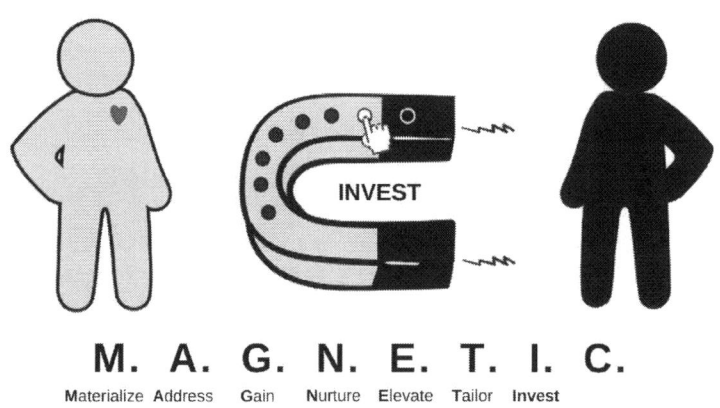

M. A. G. N. E. T. I. C.
Materialize Address Gain Nurture Elevate Tailor **Invest**

Before we get into specific techniques, strategies, and tools for improving your organic social media, let's talk high level and make sure we're all on the same page with what social media actually is.

If you don't understand what social media is at a fundamental level, it will never work for you.

Lesson #1: The key word in social media is SOCIAL.

People join networks so that they can keep up with other people—their friends, family, peers, colleagues, acquaintances, favorite entertainers, athletes, and thought leaders. Social media is a community at heart.

"the key word in SOCIAL MEDIA" is SOCIAL.

And you can't call yourself a member of any community if you don't **invest** in it.

Social media is a place where people go when they're done working. It's a place they visit while they're having a morning cup of coffee or on their lunch break. While they're sitting on the couch waiting to eat dinner after a long day at work. When they're unwinding in bed before they call it a day.

It is a place that should be easy for them to engage with whatever they want.

It's not a place where people go to learn about new tax law or read complex articles that get into the weeds about actuarial studies on financial success.

Lesson #2: Social media is not a place where people go to be sold!

People go on social media to look at pictures of dogs and babies and watch funny videos and see who got engaged and what their friends did over the weekend.

Is it a place where people go to research financial advisors? Does social media play a part in the decision-making process? Are people sold on social media? Yes, of course.

But more than that, it's a place where people go to access the things that all humans crave: Connection with others.

> No one goes on social thinking,
> "Boy, I'd sure love to book an appointment
> with an advisor today!"

If you approach social media as first and foremost a place to gather leads and assets—a place to sell—you will not only see ZERO results, but you will also alienate your ideal prospects and turn everyone else off.

Take a moment to reflect on how you show up on social.

Are you constantly pitching yourself? Approaching strangers and bombarding them with your stuff without reading the room or asking them if it's okay?

If you are, there's no way your social media strategy is working.

1. Truth Is...**There's no magic bullet to social (sorry).**

I know that many will purchase this book hoping to walk away with my recommendation on The Best Social Media Platform for Financial Advisors. I'm sorry to say that I can't give you that.

As you've probably guessed, I do personally have an affinity for a couple platforms—LinkedIn and Instagram as it currently stands. *Currently* is the key word. Even if they're my personal go-to's, I'm not going to say they're "the best."

This is the question that everyone asks: "Which social media platform is the best?"

Here's the answer:

> The best social media platform is the one that you are not only actively investing in but enjoy spending time on.

Our resident digital marketing expert Tom—the one who works with A-List celebrities and fills stadiums for household names—once had a client who saw a serious lead-flow from Snapchat and wanted Tom to look at it.

The client really wanted to build a massive audience on Instagram, but couldn't rationalize why his casual, daily Snapchat activity was getting more traction than his Instagram page.

When they dug deeper, the difference-maker wasn't related to the algorithm or to the content flavor of the month. It was the fact that the client posted on Snapchat *eight times a day*.

As for his pages on other platforms? He was posting two or three times a week, if at all.

Tom told him, "The reason you're getting the most engagement, leads, and sales on Snapchat is because you're **using it the most**."

Which platform do YOU gravitate towards?

Which social media communities do you find yourself effortlessly investing time and energy into?

Whichever it is, there is a strong possibility your ideal client and demographic is on there as well.

Now, there *are* things to consider from platform to platform. So, I asked Tom if that advice changed when you consider how much of our industry is focused on (pre-)retirees.

The question was, "Let's say an advisor wanted to focus on and put the most work in on TikTok, but his target demographic is 65 plus. Do you still feel like that's a solid social media platform to invest in?"

Here's what he said:

"I know a guy who's probably about 60 years old and is a TikTok Rockstar, making at least six figures selling financial advice.

Let's just say 2 percent of the total TikTok audience is in the demographic that's preparing for retirement. How many people does that put you in front of?"

Well, as of August 2020, 7.1 percent of TikTok users are 50 years old and up. With a user base of 100 million monthly active users in the United States, that's seven million people.

Not exactly abysmal.

Besides, and again, wouldn't you rather create your own lane? Wouldn't you rather compete on a platform that you enjoy spending time on?

2. Truth Is...**There is a method to the madness and it's called the algorithm.**

Every single platform on social media is engineered, optimized, and constantly re-evaluated for positive user experience, which is a super "nice" way to refer to a "dopamine-driven feedback loop."

What positive user experience looks like and how it's enforced via the algorithm varies, depending on the platform.

The algorithm is a set of rules that determines who sees what content. It decides what content shows up on people's timelines and for how long.

Understanding the algorithms on social media at a basic level is the difference-maker in your success on social media.

> If you actively study the algorithm,
> it's nothing short of *magic*.

Most social media platforms do not show content based on what was the most recently posted, but instead show what the platform thinks you'll find to be the most engaging.

YES, timing your posts is important—which we'll get to in a sec—but timing isn't everything. You must play to "the powers that be" if you want your content to capture maximum attention and achieve maximum engagement.

Like the criteria you may look at to decide which investments to allocate to, social media platforms look for characteristics such as:

- Whether the post is a picture or video
- Whether there is a link included
- Whether there are any hashtags—and if so, how many?
- The relationship between the user and the person sharing the content. Are they friends or family? Is this someone the user might know in real life?
- How other people responding to the post
- Whether the user usually engages with this person or content via likes, comments, or direct messages

Without studying the algorithm and catering to it, even if you have the most interesting and valuable content on the Internet, you won't get much traction.

Chapter 12

THE ALGORITHM

Cross the algorithm in the wrong ways and the robots behind the scenes will make sure your content is essentially buried and therefore goes unseen.

Think of it this way:

You should be focused on building relationships with *two* parties when you're online. Yes, your audience is one of them, but the other relationship you'll need to invest in and develop is your relationship with *the algorithm.*

What does the algorithm want from your relationship? Your help bringing users back to spend time on the platform day in and day out and keeping them there.

Unfortunately, platforms don't spell out their algorithms. It's not entirely transparent information.

We must work with what we've got, which means relying on experience, constantly testing, taking advantage of insights from experts who study the algorithms, and watching for the occasional announcement on major changes from the head honchos of the platform.

Don't worry, it's not a daily change, but about once a year you can expect each platform's algorithm to adjust based on changing views of what they think is interesting, valuable, and relevant.

Assuming you want people to see your posts, make a note to periodically hit up Google and see if there's anything that has changed that you should be mindful of in the future.

3. Truth Is...**Social media algorithms mirror the human algorithm.**

Your organic content is most likely going to be seen by your immediate connections and potentially, their connections as well. Organic reach, meaning how much free viewership you generate, is something that continues to decrease as social media platforms look to increase their revenue.

Since many social media platforms show the most relevant (not the most recent) content, there are systems that allow the platforms to essentially gauge the relevance (and quality) of your stuff.

Is there a way to cheat the system?

No. Sorry. Relationships online take time, just like they do in real life. Can't cheat the human algorithm. :)

Regardless of the platform, there are seven keys to social media success. Study, practice, and test these seven concepts consistently for an extended period to drastically improve your firm's outcomes on social media.

1ST KEY TO SUCCESS ON SOCIAL:
Know How Your Content is Scored

In the world of social media, think of likes, comments, and shares as your currency.

This is an oversimplification, as the algorithm is looking at this data on a much deeper level and evaluating things like the length of comments, whether people are corresponding back and forth, or whether or not they're tagging their friends.

However, your goal is to rack up as many points on a post as possible, therefore telling the algorithm that this content should be served to a greater number of your audience.

2ND KEY TO SUCCESS ON SOCIAL:
Don't Sleep on Golden Hour

When you post, your content will initially only be rolled out to a small portion of your audience—let's say 10 percent. And any response (or lack of response) that occurs during the Golden Hour (or the first hour that your content is live), will determine the lifespan of your post.

If there's a ton of activity on your post during its Golden Hour—a.k.a., you get a lot of engagement—your post will continue to do well for days and, in some cases, for weeks to come.

But if that first hour is a dud? RIP.

Want to know an easy way to set yourself up for success during your Golden Hour? Make sure you're posting when people are online.

There is an insane amount of data out there about the best times to post, and they're not always consistent with results. The "best time to post" also varies across platforms, and then again across various demographics on the same platform.

Like anything else, you're going to want to test your Golden Hour. For example, where is your audience located? The things people are doing at 5 p.m. in Washington, D.C. are very different from what they're doing at 2 p.m. in Los Angeles.

The best time to post for someone who serves a specific region is going to be different for a purely virtual advisor who isn't tied to any specific area or state.

Using Eastern Standard Time (EST) is a solid rule of thumb when you want to hit people in different time zones. Many industries, including ours, are tied to EST. And nearly 50 percent of the US population is in EST.

Considering that 80 percent of the US population lives in either EST or Central Standard Time (CST), finding a happy medium between the two could also make sense.

Really, I don't want to dissuade you from testing, but common sense can provide guidance about where to start. For example, if you're targeting older people or working professionals, it probably doesn't make sense to post at 1 a.m. when most people are sleeping.

Also, if you're still working at 1 a.m., you should stop. :)

3ʳᴰ KEY TO SUCCESS ON SOCIAL: Personal Pages > Business Pages

Social media platforms will always prioritize posts coming from *individuals* over companies and brands. They want to serve content from people you know, follow, and regularly interact with (and make companies pay for engagement and run ads).

However, having a business account or page is a good idea, and if you want to run advertisements and paid content campaigns on a major social media site, it's a necessity. You can't put money behind the content you're sharing from an individual account.

If someone sees your ad and clicks back to your business page, you don't want them seeing a lot of outdated, uninteresting stuff.

With that said, don't expect an insane amount of eyeballs on the organic content you share on a business page. Your highest engagement and viewership will come from what's shared on a personal page.

This doesn't mean your business page will be nothing more than a bump on a log. If you signal to the algorithm that it's a business page that people are engaging with by driving people to it and incentivizing them to comment, your business page will get more reach, a.k.a.:

- → Post on your personal page
- → Share it on your business page
- → Use your business page to engage with content from other people/pages

The comments and responses that corporations and celebrities leave on content sometimes draw more attention to their page than the content itself! *Hellooo,*comment marketing. We'll talk more about this shortly.

On your business pages, a.k.a. the account you run advertisements from, consider setting posts up to represent you as an individual. People do business with people, so attach your name instead of your practice's name.

Have a big team with several producing advisors? Consider naming the page something like "Your Friends at [Company Name]."

4th KEY TO SUCCESS ON SOCIAL:
Embrace New Platform Features

When a platform rolls out a new feature, maybe they've added live video or a stories section, use it. You will be rewarded for entertaining new features and being a supporter of the latest and greatest idea.

Be an early adopter to new features. Try them out, see if they work for you. The algorithm will do its part to get you the eyeballs.

5th KEY TO SUCCESS ON SOCIAL:
Be Wary of Posting Links

Remember that, above all, these social media platforms are money-making enterprises. They are not charities.

The primary way the platforms make money is by collecting revenue from people who spend money running ads.

The more effective the ads are, the more companies will continue to spend money on the platform to place those advertisements, a.k.a. more revenue.

That's why the algorithm aims to serve you content that will keep you scrolling.

The longer you're online, the more ads you'll see.

When you post a link, a.k.a. send people away from the platform, you basically tell the Almighty Algorithm that you don't want it to make money. Posting links is a surefire way to make sure your content is buried. Your fantastic content will be doomed the second you insert the URL to an external site.

This is unfortunate because links are a cornerstone to most of the "done-for-you" social media content promoted by the big companies in our industry.

Chapter 12

But—nine times out of ten—almost exclusively sharing links to outside stuff is *not* a good strategy.

This strategy is basically you repetitively telling the platform you don't want them to make any money. And you will be punished for it.

Sometimes you can't get around it if the gold is on an external site. If/when that's the case, there are a couple of workarounds.

Let's say you're trying to grow your podcast audience, which you also capture on video and upload to YouTube.

Instead of sharing the link to YouTube, you could have the video repurposed like we talked about in Chapter 10 into a small clip of a powerful moment on the show or a cliffhanger. In your copy and in the video, prompt them to head to YouTube (or wherever you host your show).

I did this for a podcast interview I did with our Diet Coke-craving friend Daniel Crosby on his show *Standard Deviations* in December of 2021. I recorded my side of the interview, chopped it up, and directed users on LinkedIn to listen to the full show.

Despite the show going live on December 17, this strategy of adding value, creating curiosity via a preview, and directing them to the show *without* posting a link helped make this his most downloaded episode of the entire year. There were only 14 days left in 2021.

Won't take all the credit though. It probably (/definitely) helps that Dan has one of the most prominent voices in the industry.

 A NOTE ON YOUTUBE: YouTube is a social media site and they're in competition with all the others. Another social media site is not the best place to grow your YouTube audience.

Businesses will want to run ads on the platforms with the most users and engagement because they hold the most opportunities to generate revenue. Again, more ads, more profitability for the social media platform.

Platforms want native videos, a.k.a. videos that are uploaded directly to the site as an "original." Take whatever you thought was super interesting and valuable about whatever you wanted to share, replace the link with an image, and use your own words to tell the story and add color.

There's no shame in referring to a source if you're including your take and delivering the value to your audience. That's content curation at its finest.

6TH KEY TO SUCCESS ON SOCIAL: Avoid Mass Tagging

You may hurt your engagement more than you help it when you tag a thousand people on all your posts hoping they like or comment on it.

If you're doing this, stop.

One—The algorithm can tell that you're taking a shortcut.

Two—If you're tagging a big enough page or person aiming to tap into their audience, you're probably not the only person trying to tag them and get them to engage. a.k.a., they will not take the action you want them to, and you may be simultaneously rubbing the wrong way by cluttering their notifications.

They're not getting any dopamine by you tagging them simply because you want something from them. They're human too.

7th KEY TO SUCCESS ON SOCIAL:
Be Wary of Canned Content

You're out of your mind if you think the algorithms don't know when the same link, image, or text is getting shared by 10,000 different people.

It knows. Your content will get dumped in the spam category and you will be punished.

Not only do I see it every day, but I've experienced it personally.

In my early industry social media days, one of my failed experiments was using one of the major third-party content companies.

Not only did the canned content get ZERO likes or comments, but when I *would* post personal content—things like pictures of me and my family over holidays or celebrating big milestones—those didn't get any engagement either. I had burned the bridge with the Facebook algorithm.

As far as the algorithm was concerned, I was a spammer with nothing unique or valuable to say. Womp, womp.

Think about it.

Social media platforms are the most relevant and interesting when content is based on human experiences and unique perspectives. When people start discussions that bring people together as well as— let's be honest—push people apart.

When the social media platforms see that 15,000 people all posted the same link at the same time on the same day from an outside service, you are basically telling the algorithm that you're not there for the right reasons.

Hopefully, you are. If so, use your voice, make it yours, and watch what happens.

4. Truth Is...You can't just post and wait for people to come to you.

Let's go back to that scale of 1 to 10 for prospect engagement.

On social media, a one would be someone seeing your content simply because the algorithm served it to them (versus them seeking it out). No clue who you are, not a follower, no connection.

A 10 would be someone who has been following you for a while and actively likes and comments on your stuff.

When someone's at a 10, they'll take the logical next step.

On social media, the logical next step is NOT an appointment. It's to get to a point where if you send them a message on the platform where they're already engaging, they'll send you one back.

That's it.

And then you're back to that scale of 1 to 10, and they're a one again. All they did was message you back. Now you need to take that response and turn it into a back-and-forth conversation that eventually becomes a phone call or text convo.

> It's not just about building trust on their timeline.
> It's about building trust in their *inbox*.

The same way you would for an email or text. The more conversations you can take off the timeline and into your inbox through real social media relationship equity, the more people will pop out of the bottom of your funnel as a client.

Turn Off All Automated Messaging

Please do not use automated messaging sequences. People can tell when messages are automated. I promise. And everyone hates them. Including me. Probably you, too.

Put yourself in your audience's shoes. How turned off would you be if you left your job or the workforce, and you got spammed by not one, but three or four random advisors reaching out with a generic message wondering if you've decided what you want to do with your 401k? Someone you know nothing about? And appears to know nothing about you?

It just doesn't work.

Remember, we have to capture people's attention and start building rapport way before the decision point. You want to build that relationship before they even leave their company, so there's some trust established if you ever decide to reach out.

And you don't want to piss off your audience—your relationships—along the way.

Who wants to advocate for a financial advisor to their friends or family if they perceive you're not willing to take the two seconds to personalize a message about one of the most important aspects of one's entire life? That their friend or family member would get the same canned message as everyone else?

There needs to be a human touch.

 FRIENDLY FYI: Using bots of ANY KIND on ANY PLATFORM will get you kicked off. Maybe not immediately, but one day. Remember, the algorithm KNOWS. There are no shortcuts.

Comment Marketing

A lot of time when we talk about content on social media, our minds go right to the pictures, videos, and information we share.

These things are important. But consider this: Your comments, messages, and the way that you engage with *other* people's stuff also counts as content and are important factors to a comprehensive content strategy.

It is not all about you!

You should be just as focused on commenting, engaging, and messaging with other people—if not more—than posting your own content.

This is a lesser known, but highly legitimate strategy, known as *comment marketing.*

This isn't so much of a hack as it is a necessity. The idea is not to comment on other people's stuff to promote your stuff and generate leads; it is simply to be social. If you're actively social on social media consistently, you will see your followers and content engagement increase over time, which is when the snowball effect kicks in.

And let's be realistic. You cannot build a community of like-minded people and raving fans without being an active participant in the conversation. Invest in the fellow members of your community—not just yourself.

It seems like common sense, but only 1 in 50 advisors who say that they believe engaging with other people is as important as posting their own stuff, actually DO IT.

If you are one of the other 49 advisors, I don't blame you for not engaging. It's hard to automate and scale.

But, if you're just starting out and your content isn't sparking too many conversations (yet), taking part in conversations that are already happening will eventually increase the engagement on your content.

Think of it this way:

Your comments on other people's stuff *also* count as content.

Make the most of your comments. Provide value, say something interesting, inject some humor. Afraid your sense of humor or perspective will scare people off who aren't picking up what you're putting down? Don't be. Magnets attract and repel, remember?

If you're feeling froggy, add some of those five-star comments onto your competitors' posts to gain exposure to their audience in a passive, positive way.

Time-block at least 30 minutes a day to invest in your social media connections and water your networks' grass.

If that isn't time that you can commit to putting in, you can also have someone on your team or a virtual assistant do the job for you—just make sure that they know your voice and value-add!

Social Media Algorithms Follow the Human Algorithm

Will social media algorithms reward you for commenting, messaging, while sharing your own content on the feed?

Absolutely!

You're telling the algorithm that you are contributing to a greater user experience, which means creating relationships and having authentic conversations.

And check it out. The platform—whether it's LinkedIn, Facebook, Instagram, whatever—is going to jump in when it sees a connection forming and will grease the wheels for the new relationship.

The algorithm essentially says, "Wait a second. These two people might know each other. And if they don't, maybe they should? Let's play matchmaker and increase their exposure to one another to see if we can bring these people together because that's what keeps people on our platform."

But honestly, it's not all about the social media algorithm.

> There's a more important (and powerful) algorithm at play: *The Human Algorithm.*

Just like in a real-life conversation or relationship, if you make it a point to show people appreciation, affirmation, and essentially provide the dopamine rush we get when we receive likes and comments, they will return the favor. The algorithm's job, more than anything, is to reinforce the social aspect of social media by acknowledging the human algorithm.

Study what the most popular pages and people do on that platform and try to improve your own profile, content, and messaging so that your

Chapter 12

page is the best page for your ideal client to follow and engage with, period. The most popular pages aren't the most popular pages on the platform by accident.

Start with one social media network, master it, and build an audience.

Then, to protect yourself from investing in a platform that falls out of favor or gets shut down, find a second platform.

Think about who you're serving and which platform you'll have the most fun **investing** in and start there. The Human Algorithm will do the rest.

Next Steps & Resources You Can Use *Today*

You know what? There's an eighth key to social media success that I (unfortunately) learned the hard way. Avoid making the same mistake and get the full story at: www.truthaboutdm.com/kristinsmistake

Chapter 13

Connecting the Dots

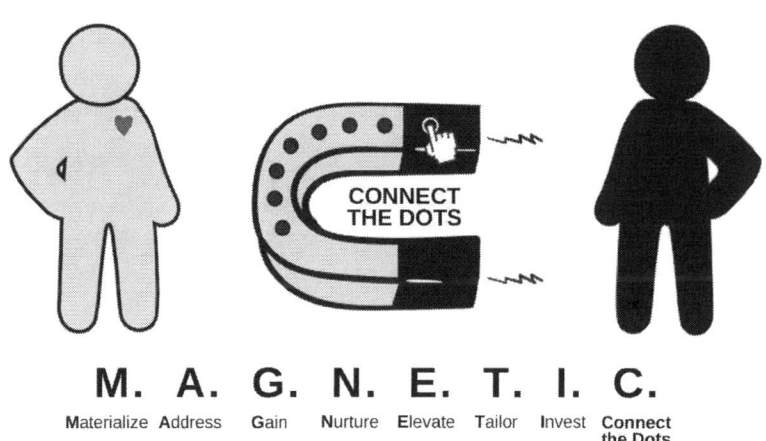

The advisors who are ahead of the pack have several marketing funnels running at the same time.

This is called marketing diversification.

> Just like you wouldn't put all your eggs in one basket using one individual fund, investment, or product, you shouldn't be reliant on one single marketing funnel.

Diversification was the difference between the advisors who thrived in 2020 and those who didn't.

The ones who thrived were not overly reliant on live events that led to face-to-face meetings. They had other marketing strategies and winning slot machines they could focus on while their live events were temporarily rendered useless.

But diversification is not enough.

Just like a financial plan has diversification inside of it, the value of having a plan is the *comprehensive, coordinated effort.* The individual pieces complement and account for the rest.

It's not just about your lead magnets.

Or your website.

Or the email and text sequences.

Or your paid campaigns or what you post on social media.

It's not about individual activities firing sporadically.

The best advisors not only have several ways to enter their funnel, but they are also coordinated and consistent from the inside out.

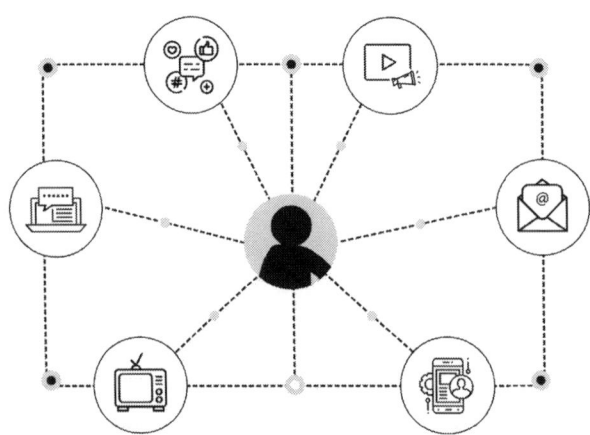

Those advisors can do what every single advisor in the industry should seek to achieve if they want to be the go-to firm in the future and avoid getting left behind: Omnipresence in their marketing.

Omnipresence is about **connecting the dots**.

1. Truth Is…**Omnipresence literally means that you're everywhere.**

The office in New England referenced earlier literally has *18 separate ways* to enter its funnel. The 18 points of entry are diversified enough to capture attention regardless of where a prospect is in their life or in their readiness to hire an advisor.

At the same time, because of their packaged process, their marketing is also congruent enough to keep that attention, show up consistently, and speed up the journey from being *aware* to being *ready to act*.

Here's an overview of what that looks like for a few of their value-adds and opportunities for engagement.

Their book is:

- ✓ On their website
- ✓ Promoted at seminars
- ✓ Repurposed as an e-book offered in a paid ad campaign
- ✓ In your mailbox within 24 hours of booking your first appointment

They leverage their podcast by:

- ✓ Putting it on their website
- ✓ Including new episodes in their email campaigns
- ✓ Repurposing clips as organic social media content
- ✓ Repurposing clips for paid advertisements

Their TV Segments:

- ✓ Airs at different times on various major networks
- ✓ Prompts their audience to sign up for webinars
- ✓ Offer a copy of their book
- ✓ Plug a lead generating quiz
- ✓ Are repurposed for social media

And their content strategy:

- ✓ Includes both paid and organic content
- ✓ Is repurposed across several social media platforms
- ✓ Is shared not just by the firm, but their team

Because they understand the importance of connecting the dots, their content marketing showcases their:

- ✓ Seminars
- ✓ Client events
- ✓ New podcast episodes
- ✓ Articles and blogs
- ✓ Team and culture
- ✓ TV segments

(Which, by the way, all speak to the same packaged process and value proposition.)

And it doesn't stop there. Their diversified funnel *also* includes:

- ✓ SEO & Google
- ✓ Live events (at several locations in town and in surrounding regions)
- ✓ TV (on different stations)
- ✓ Client referrals
- ✓ COI referrals
- ✓ Emails

Chapter 13

- ✓ Webinars
- ✓ Client events—in person
- ✓ Client events—virtual
- ✓ Monthly magazine ads

I think you get it.

I know that not all of these are digital, but half of them are.

This list also passively points to the importance of coordinating your marketing efforts—not just the ones you do online, but those that happen *offline* as well.

The collective presence and coordination results in a true machine.

Remember Michael, the 32-year-old from Chapter 6? The one who said the most important hire he's ever made was an appointment setter? The one who started his firm from scratch three years ago and is now bringing on $60 million annually in new assets? He also has over ten different ways of getting clients. Every single one of them connects to the other.

 WINK, WINK: Michael also fills his educational events using custom, paid ad campaigns from experts like Tom to get seminar registrants at $42 a head. ;)

I know that some of you are either a long way off from bringing on $60 to $300 million a year or simply have no interest in getting that big.

But, if you're here, in the last chapter of this book…I know you want better results in your marketing.

This is the absolute endgame. Connect the dots and become omnipresent.

What Next?

Instead of thinking about all the activities you aren't currently doing in your digital marketing, I want you to take a deep breath, relax your shoulders, and know that this is where I meet you where you are.

What do you already have?

And what small things can we do inside of those marketing assets to leverage them and build a foundation for the future, both for the experience of your audience and the workflows inside your team?

We're going to use your website as an example. I feel comfortable assuming you have a website.

First, I'll paint a different picture of how to think about omnipresent marketing, and once we've applied it to something as foundational as your website, we'll talk about other ways to bring it all together.

In this chapter I will teach you how to be *everywhere.*

2. Truth Is...Omnipresence is like being a marketing socialite and the best host in town.

Let's go to imaginary land for a second and pretend you just LOVE to throw parties. It's your thing. All year, every year.

The time comes to begin planning your annual Christmas extravaganza. The party of the year. You're in the holiday spirit and you're going *big*. Just like you always do.

You invite your family, of course.

And your significant other if you have one.

Chapter 13

You invite your best friends, who will bring their significant others as well. This includes that one friend who just got out of a terrible relationship and is bringing their brand-new girlfriend to the party so everyone can meet them.

In-between every event on the annual calendar, you're striking up conversations with new potential friends and future guests everywhere you go. You like to maintain strong relationships with your existing people, but you also love bringing in new faces.

Also included on the guest list: Your favorite coworkers, maybe your boss, your old coworkers, some new friends, and some people who seem to have potential to be friends one day, for example, the people in your workout class.

Everyone. Bringing people together is your favorite part about being the Host with the Most.

Most of the people you expect to say yes will RSVP as they always do, and many of your newer friends say they'll be there when they get the invite as well.

"For sure! Sounds great. I'll be there."

You've got yourself one hell of a guest list.

You want everyone to be comfortable, and you're going to do your best to make everyone feel at home, but ultimately, you know how these things go. You know you can't please everyone. Plus, the event is just as much for *you* as it is for everyone else.

You'll do your best to make sure that new girlfriend who seems nice *enough* to walk out with good things to say, even though you're disgusted when you see she keeps using the same fingers she's licking after she helps herself to the small bowls of nuts to grab more.

Overall, guests will leave your home happy for one of two reasons:

One—It was the best party they've ever been to. Because they can't wait 'til next year's Christmas party to hang out with you again, they're texting you the next morning asking what you're doing on New Year's Eve.

Two—They gave it a shot, appreciated all your efforts, and the food was amazing, yet they slipped out and told their significant other, "Thank goodness we left when we did," knowing that they tried, but will not return next year.

Works for you.

That's magnetic omnipresence.

Omnipresence is not about the *one* individual tool or *one* specific stage a member of your audience is at. It's bigger than that.

It's not the lights you put on the tree or what kinds of cookies you had out or where the cars parked in the driveway.

It's making every single person, regardless of where they were in their relationship with you before they showed up, feel at home and have a good enough time to want to come back next year.

It's also understanding that those who don't want to come back *won't* come back because it's not for them. And you're a-okay with that.

For these people who you don't bother inviting back next year, there's no love lost. At the end of the day, they can respect you for doing the darn thing, inviting them into your home, and knowing that there *are* people who had the time of their life.

And you can appreciate them for giving you a shot, and not putting themselves in the situation to be a Debbie Downer at the next one.

It's your whole audience. Your entire guest lists. The ongoing calendar of events and every interaction with other potentially like-minded people in between.

3. Truth Is...**Omnipresence begins by optimizing what you already have.**

Let's talk about that website of yours.

Your website is not likely to show up on your marketing ROI reports as a tool that drives a meaningful number of new leads or business your way—but it's worth drawing attention to.

Your website is a perfect example of a digital marketing asset that should operate as one of your many big Digital Marketing Parties that feeds your omnipresent, digital marketing beast.

Your audience will enter your funnel/see your stuff, and in this case your website, at different places in their readiness to work with an advisor. Same with your social media content, podcast, invitations to your events, all of it.

> New members of your audience will join your marketing universe at different stages.

Be a good host in your marketing party and make people feel at home and meet them where they are.

When there is any seriousness in exploring whether they're going to work with you, they're going to head to your website. It's inevitable.

I'm about to give you a ton of great tips to take your website to the next level.

But honestly, this is not just about your website.

It's about everything else connected to it and what it represents.

The lens I am about to provide for you to look at your website can and should be applied to every single place that you show up, both online and offline.

Let Them Know They're in the Right Place

First things first: Make sure you're capturing the attention of the *right* people. Boldly declare who your company specifically serves and why prospects should care.

You have eight seconds to get your audience's attention. Do it in eight seconds.

Just like the Tito's new ad campaign I mentioned in Chapter 4. Vodka for dog people.

If you're a dog person, and you want to be known as the advisor for dog people, say that.

"We help dog people achieve their financial goals."

 LET'S JUST PLAY THIS OUT: As a dog lover, and as corny as this example is, I think this has legs. Health care for a dog would need to be considered in your retirement income planning. What happens to the dog if you pass away? Don't you still want your dog to have a yard, even after you downsize in retirement? There's so much there. Plus, you make sure website visitors know they can bring their dog into the office and put a picture of your pup on your website as an "honorary staff member" and it's game over.

In all seriousness, if your niche isn't as deep or hyper-specific like Adam's or Derek's from Chapter 3 (#goals), you still need to call "them" out, whoever "they" are.

After that, consider saving everyone some time and additionally be explicit about who is NOT a good fit for your firm.

From there, let those ideal clients know how great it is that they've arrived.

Instead of listing out or having paragraphs of info about the nuances of each service, focus on your super specific value proposition.

Package all those services that you offer into one proprietary branded package with a trademark on it.

We do this thing. For these people. Who are at this stage of their life. Who want this thing more than anything. And here's what our packaged process, that you can't get anywhere else, means for them and their ability to live happier lives.

When you use simple, clear, concise language that stays out of the weeds, you free up a lot of space to add value and bring their attention to that next step and engage with you further.

Provide Opportunities for Them to Engage with You Throughout the Funnel

Next, think about how you can engage with them throughout the entire funnel and give them opportunities to do that through your website. Here are some examples of content that will help move them through the funnel:

Top of Funnel:

- → What will they gain by signing up for your emails? Give them a preview and provide a CTA so they can sign up
- → Include quotes, or even better, make it possible to download show notes you're your podcast, radio, or tv show
- → Don't just tell them you have social media profiles—put your social media content on your website and let that live feed be your blog

Middle of Funnel:

- → Are you running webinars? If so, provide a short, valuable preview as a teaser with a prompt to catch the full virtual event
- → If you're running live events, include a video clip of your biggest mic drop moment alongside the calendar of events and actual photos from previous seminars or celebrations

Bottom of Funnel:

- → Provide a preview of a sample financial plan with an easy-to-digest before and after case study that highlights common problems you see
- → Give an example what questions people often have and let them know you're on the other side of the phone if they have their own quick question they want to run by you via text, phone, or email
- → Proactively address any objections and plant questions that they may not have already considered to manage expectations and showcase your value using conversationally answered FAQs

In the process, look for ways to call out where they are and what they should do next:

"HEY, are you here checking us out because you received one of our event invitations? We're so glad you're here! You can watch a quick 30 second preview HERE."

Will everyone be on your website because they were invited to an event? Nope. But now they know you do events and people are looking you up because of it.

And maybe, instead of simply leaving your site, they'll watch the preview. They'll make a mental note to check back and look at your event calendar in nine months when they retire and will begin listening to your podcast in the meantime because you prompted that too.

Look for ways to create a personal connection

Your audience will spend the most time on your website on your "About Me" page. Most advisors have a photo in a suit and tie, accompanied by a long bio full of credentials and a quick sentence or two at the bottom about what they like to do in their spare time and how many kids they have.

Let's flip that. The thing that brings people in and pushes them over the edge is their ability to connect with you. Replace your headshot with something a bit more informal, turn that bio into a story, and throw in some pictures of you with your family.

Even the couples you work with will approach you at different levels of interest. Make it easy for the wife to show her husband your website and say, "Look, babe! They're just like us."

Help them visualize what it means to work together

If your knee was bothering you, and you realize the pain wasn't going away on its own, you'll decide it's time to visit the doctor. It won't be a hard trigger for you to pull.

Why?

Because you know what it's like to be at a doctor's office. You know how doctors work and have an idea of what the process of getting that knee fixed will look like.

You can imagine checking in, showing your insurance card, getting called back, and being delivered to a room to answer some quick questions before the nurse is replaced by the doctor.

After the appointment, you'll follow the path to the check-out desk, book your next appointment to follow up, and leave with a sticker or a prescription already on the way to the pharmacy.

For financial advisors, it's different.

The process, the products, the plan can vary *so much* from one advisor to the next. On top of that, you cannot hold, taste, smell, or test a financial plan. It's not tangible.

People will be much more likely to book an appointment with you one day if you can help provide visual prompts and points of reference so that they can literally imagine themselves meeting with you.

Have an engaging video tour of your office on your website and switch the stock photos out with real photos of you and your team in your natural settings.

If you don't have a video or functional high-quality photos just yet, throw out the stock images of the old couple on the sailboat anyway.

No one trusts or pays attention to stock photos, and our industry is saturated with them.

No, I mean, like ACTUALLY visualize what it means to WORK TOGETHER:

Instead of having a list of your vague four-step process, including a discovery meeting, a strategy session, implementation, and then monitoring, spell out exactly what that means.

How long are the meetings? What is covered? What does the prospect need to bring? Do they have a choice between virtual or in person? What happens after the meeting?

And then take it one step further. Clearly break down and define what it would look like if they were to become a client.

What happens in the first 30 days?
What about the first 90?
First year?

What will you do?
What kind of commitment is this?
What's in it for them?

Spell it out.

> Stress and friction are more about the *uncertainty* than the outcome.

Provide Social Proof:

When we talked about lead magnets in Chapter 8, I promised we'd come back to testimonials. Testimonials and creating social proof is *so* important.

Here's an opportunity I feel confident sharing—without running the risk of publishing a book that's immediately outdated or giving you terrible advice: If you're licensed, ask your compliance team what their take is on using Google reviews as testimonials.

If it's possible, figure out what your compliance team is comfortable with you doing/saying to generate as many Google reviews as possible and put those bad boys on your website (and wherever you can).

After that, and before you go to bed tonight, say a prayer that one day soon, our industry will allow us to go deeper and do more with testimonials. I'll be right there with you.

No one's getting on the amusement park's new roller coaster until they know someone else has ridden it before. Even better if you know they not only survived the ride but got right back in line to do it again.

Now, let's say—worst case scenario—testimonials in any way, shape, or form is an absolute no-go for your team.

You do still have options.

For example, I am THRILLED to share a brilliant idea from Joseph Cammayo, an awesome advisor (and human!) in my LinkedIn community, based on how he satisfies the visual "itch" your audience has to look for testimonials.

As mentioned, your audience is trained to look for insights on the experience of a product or service when they look them up online.

Even if they go to your website and don't actively think "Where are the testimonials?", there's often a subconscious sense that something's *missing*.

Check out what Joseph and his team have done to satisfy that itch.

On his website, he has the scrolling section that visually indicates that you're being presented with testimonials. But, instead of *client* quotes, his firm features quotes from their *team*.

The quote above came from one of the other lead advisors at the firm.

Joseph's is, *"Financial Planning is bringing the future into the present so that you can do something about it now."*

Another says, *"It's my goal to make sure every client feels heard and understood."*

10/10 use of space on their homepage. Even if they're not testimonials from clients, it is a testimonial of the team's heart, intentions, and what you can hold them accountable to.

Other workarounds include:

- Data-driven trends that indicate movement among your ideal audience that will reinforce that they're not alone and the value of your service
- Stories(!!!)
- Hypothetical case studies that represent your ideal client and their specific goals, pain points, future crossroads, and potential outcomes

Put your custom pixel on the back end of your website:

Boom. Now you too can start running retargeting advertisements to people who visited your site and follow them around on the Internet.

Congratulations, and welcome to the dark side.

Don't give them opportunities to get lost:

Remember how I said landing pages differ from websites because they are only one page? And because there's no extra "stuff" and places to get lost, they're better at driving conversions than websites?

That's the case for most websites.

But…What if you turned your website into a landing page? It would be a long landing page with varying calls to action, but one page is always better than five.

I promise, you don't need all the STUFF on your website. You *definitely* don't need the calculators.

People just want to know that you're legit, what you're about, and if you might be able to help them.

For you? You just want them to take the next step.

4. Truth Is…**You can lead the horse to water, but only the right horse will drink.**

To be omnipresent in your digital marketing, you have to be in all places at all times.

But just because you meet your audience everywhere they are, doesn't mean that they're paying attention.

Let's use Coca-Cola as an example. Coca-Cola is the epitome of having an omnipresent brand. In just 24 hours, I've encountered Coca-Cola as a product or through their marketing four times. And no, that's not including Daniel Crosby's viral post.

There was a commercial, there's Coca-Cola in the fridge at our office, it was on a table in front of a friend in a picture she posted on social media, and at the checkout line at the grocery store.

It's everywhere.

But it's not *relevant* to me because I don't drink soda. I can only tell you how many times I encountered Coca-Cola's brand in the past day because I edited this chapter to report back.

Any other day? In any real-life situation where I'm not trying to give an example for a book? I just don't see it. It's not that I'm *offended* by how close I am to Coca-Cola at any given moment or my level of exposure to the brand. I'd just never drink it. I don't pay any attention to it.

Your message means nothing if you fail to:

- → Know your audience
- → Know what's personal to them
- → Show up in as many places where they are as consistently as possible

I may not be in Coca-Cola's ideal audience, but there are TONS of people who are. When they see the commercial, they think, "Man, a Coke sounds really good." When they hit the gas station to fill their tank, they'll buy a can of Coke.

Coca-Cola isn't out here trying to change my mind and convince me that Coca-Cola will support my healthy lifestyle. Maybe a little, with their zero-calorie options, but I'm not in that audience either. Even then, they aren't trying to tell me that their version of "no sugar" is the same as a natural alternative. They know there are many people just like me who are really focused on a clean diet.

Coca-Cola doesn't mind. There are enough people out there who are in its ideal audience. And lucky for both the company *and* that ideal audience, Coca-Cola is omnipresent.

Remember that picture I took at the McDonald's in Thailand from Chapter 4? LOL I did not order or eat anything. Way too much authentic Thai food I couldn't get anywhere else. Plus…I'd pick Thai food over McDonald's, even in the states, any day of the week.

But, seeing Mr. Ronald McDonald posing with a traditional Thai greeting at one of the many McDonald's I saw in Thailand, I had to take a photo. Blew my mind.

I can't imagine how much crazier it would've been if I was the type of person who LOVED Big Macs, was struggling with spicy Thai food, and found a McDonald's on the other side of the world.

It would be a refuge!

How can you create that same experience in *your* business?

Imagine if an ideal client connected with you, encountered your value proposition, and had an opportunity to engage with you and get your help on solving a problem four times, four different ways in ONE DAY.

Especially in a sea of same-ness—where you're the only advisor that actually speaks to what they care about?

If this seems like a lot, I get it.

I'm not saying you need to capture your audience's four different ways every single day.

I'm not telling you to spend as much money on marketing as Coca-Cola (LOL).

But you also *don't* need to be a firm bringing on tens or hundreds of millions of dollars to create a sense of omnipresence for your ideal client.

Approach this endeavor to omnipresence NOT by playing the unwinnable, daily game of "marketing Whac-A-Mole," but by simply thinking like a CEO.

When you identify your niche, it's SO EASY to find them online. For example, you can:

1. Find online communities, for example Facebook groups, based on affinities
2. Create content for online publications that your ideal client or niche is likely to read

3. Understand what social media platform they're likely to use by looking at demographics and lifestyle data
4. Understand what capacity they might have for different forms of content.
5. Run targeted advertisements based on specific interests, demographics, and industries

If you're consistently showing up where they are, they'll eventually find you.

Keep it simple, stay consistent, continue to diversify, and the **dots will begin to connect themselves.**

Conclusion

There are a couple next steps you'll want to take—and *no*, picking up your phone ASAP to call your website company is not one of them.

Before we get to those next steps...

Let's all take a deep breath and start saying ***"no"*** to the fire alarms go off (or you create) every time a new opportunity or shiny object comes your way.

If your goal is to master digital marketing, this is exactly the type of behavior that will hold you back and burn you out.

I know you're busy. I know you're excited to get the ball rolling. But... Let's take a beat.

> *It does not serve you or anyone else if you're constantly pulling (and reacting to) fire alarms.*

The end goal here is getting ahead. But...If everything's a fire drill...If it's not sustainable, duplicatable, or easy to pass off, how far ahead can you really get?

And if you're drowning in leads from your killer digital marketing machine but you don't have the time to serve them, what's the point?

Mindset First:

One of my biggest hopes as we conclude is that you get in the habit of approaching your digital marketing (and the business decisions about marketing in general) like a CEO.

I'm tired of talking to incredible advisors and human beings who are exhausted, burned out, and have fallen out of love with their business because they have run themselves ragged trying to do it all.

Another plaque or trophy for production *isn't* worth another year of life where you're absent from family dinners, afraid to take a vacation, and missing out on all that the world offers outside of work.

No matter where you are in your career—whether you're just starting out or if you're one of established and elite advisors who feels like something HAS TO GIVE—start with crafting a vision of your ideal future.

Look inside yourself, think about how you can de-commoditize, and get your vision right. Not just a vision for your digital marketing or business—but for your life. And then use that vision as a reference every single time you're presented with a new shiny opportunity.

If the opportunity doesn't support your ideal future, keep moving.

No more saying "yes", cutting the check, and figuring out if and how it fits as an afterthought. The less you think like an advisor looking for leads and more like a CEO looking for leverage, the easier it is to build a better business and a life with unlimited upside.

Conclusion

 FOR OLD TIME'S SAKE: Truth is, I'll go so far to say that running a good business as a financial advisor is a part of your fiduciary responsibility. You can't act with care, skill, prudence, diligence if you're burned out, everything bottlenecks on you, and you're pouring from an empty cup.

Relieve yourself of the pressure to "do more, sell more, spend more". Don't feel the need to be like "that big advisor up on stage". You're not him/her, and they're not you.

Think bigger. Dream bigger. *Do it your way.*

Commit to challenging the industry status-quo, consistently trying and testing new things, and failing fast along the way.

This is your business. Your life. You can do anything you set your mind to.

Remember: As a financial advisor, the ultimate outcome of your work is stronger families, more empowered communities, and a better world for generations to come.

Can't think of anything more inspiring than that.

Marketing Second:

As far as your digital marketing goes, there are three big takeaways from *The Truth About Digital Marketing for Financial Advisors* that you've got to keep front and center:

1. **In a highly commoditized industry and the Attention Economy, you must dial in, de-commoditize, and package your value proposition.** Nobody can do this for you. Start by looking within yourself, identifying what sets you on fire, and leaning into the humanity of your ideal advisor-client relationship. Forget the masses. Go deep or go home.

2. **Remember The CAVE Conversion Method™ and its two prerequisites**. First, know the difference between the top, middle, and bottom of a funnel and the corresponding hurdles/value-adds for your audience. Second, see the members of your audience for what they are: Human beings, not just "leads."

CAVE is all about creating emotional connections, adding massive value, and engaging with—NOT PITCHING—your audience. Applying those three, easy principles means de-mystifying and mastering the art turning strangers on the internet into clients and raving fans.

3. **The foundation of The Magnetic Digital Advisor Framework™ is all about working backwards.** Start by evaluating your firm and its unique digital marketing goals, and then create the systems and infrastructure to support your efforts. Get the right people and processes in place and watch how much easier it will be to:

- **M**aterialize more clients and growth
- **A**ddress your audience
- **G**ain new prospects and relationships
- **N**urture your budding digital relationships
- **E**levate the level of value and depth of your online relationships
- **T**ailor authentic and engaging content to your audience
- **I**nvest in your online community
- **C**onnect the dots of your diversified marketing efforts

You'll know that you've become magnetic when you're consistently attracting the people (and opportunities!) that are aligned with your values—while simultaneously protecting your time and energy from those that aren't.

👉 **GRAB THE "106 TRUTHS ABOUT DIGITAL" CHEATSHEET:** For a full list of every single key takeaway from this book, head to: www.truthaboutdm.com/106truths.

Final Words

We've talked a lot about the challenges advisors face in their digital marketing. The sub-par industry solutions, the war for attention, the hurdles for your audience.

Are they real challenges to overcome? Yes.
Will it take time? Yes.
Will you hit roadblocks? Yes.

Should these challenges scare you? Absolutely not.
If you're *slightly, maybe* intimidated, that's okay.

> The greatest, most fulfilling things in life are usually found *just outside your comfort zone.*

My hope is that, more anything, you finish this book feeling empowered.

Inspired to think outside the box and pave new paths for you, your team, and your (prospective) clients.

You guys, I want you so excited about creating a magnetic, authentic digital presence that you're ready to go outside and flip cars in the parking lot with your bare hands.

If you would've told 21-year-old Kristin having an identity crisis in her new role as an annuity wholesaler that she was only a few years away from being on tour with The Rolling Stones or close to having the *Wall Street Journal* reach out for her two cents, she would not have believed you. These things happened to me because of digital marketing.

Digital marketing can transform the way you do business and unlock opportunities beyond what you currently believe is possible.

There's unlimited upside on the table. You just have to reach out and grab it.

Kristin

KristinShea

P.S. Do You Want to Work Together? :)

I often get questions like "Can I hire you to help me with my digital marketing?" or, "Do you do any freelance consulting?".

If we're on the same page and you're wondering if I'm up for hire as in a consultative role for your digital strategy, the truth is…No.

HOWEVER. For the right advisors and teams, I may be able to offer something better.

At the end of 2020, I hit a wall. I could no longer sit back and be complacent about how many advisors—especially the top 1% of advisors—were being underserved.

So, I burned the bridges, left husband Joe (my fiancé at the time) in Northern Virginia, took our dog, and relocated to Kansas to help build a company with the sole focus of helping elite advisors solve important problems and create freedom in ways that no one else had.

When I tell you to go deep, instead of wide, I'm practicing what I preach.

My company, Triad Partners, is not for everyone—in fact we say "no" to working with firms almost 10 times more frequently than we say "yes."

As a highly exclusive business development company and IMO/FMO, protecting our community and ability to serve it is one of our biggest priorities.

Conclusion

The advisors we work with must be:

→ A players
→ Growth-focused
→ Willing to check their ego at the door

When a partnership does make sense, these types of advisors gain immediate and intimate access to an exclusive community of the industry's best advisors and the planet's greatest minds including people like Michael Hyatt, our friend and the business thought leader mentioned in Chapter 3.

Yes, digital marketing is included. But the Triad Community is bigger than that.

We help advisors build businesses that don't require them to choose between growing their firm and living their life.

Contrary to what you may have heard or experienced…You can have both.

Question is: *Do you **want** both?*

Is it a goal of yours to have a de-commoditized, systematized business with an org chart full of specialists that you can trust to maintain the growth of your firm while you take a two-week vacation with your family?

Crave relief from the demands of the industry's "conveyer belt culture"?

Looking for a partnership that treats you like 1 of 1, instead of 1 of 10,000?

Ready to not only take your business to the next level with a rejuvenated sense of purpose?

That's where we come in.

Together (if we're authentically aligned ☺), we can do one of two things:

Option 1: Have a quick phone conversation and with the goal of connecting, getting to know each other, and simply seeing if it makes sense to continue the conversation

Option 2: Jumpstart your transformation by reserving a seat at an upcoming Advisor Intensive™. This intimate and unique experience is a time for us to put our heads together and deep dive into your business. Over the course of 24 hours—which equates to 4 to 6 months of weekly coaching calls based on The Triad Transformation Track™ —we'll uncover opportunities, gain actionable insights on how to solve your firm's biggest challenges, and lay the foundation for achieving scale.

 If you think you might be a good fit, or have an interest in exploring either option, go ahead and apply today: www.truthaboutdm.com/apply.

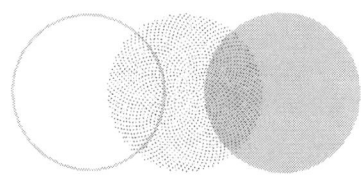

References

Andre, L. A. (2022, January 14). *109 Online Form Abandonment Statistics: 2022 Data, Trends & Impact*. Financesonline.Com. https://financesonline.com/form-abandonment-statistics/

Attention. (2015). In *APA Dictionary of Psychology* (2nd ed.). American Psychological Association. https://dictionary.apa.org/attention

Ciccarelli, D. C. (2022, January 16). *What Is the Most Effective Length for a TV Commercial?* Voices. https://www.voices.com/blog/effective_length_for_tv_commercials/

DELGADO, M. D. (2018, April 17). *6 Steps for Avoiding Online Form Abandonment*. The Manifest. https://themanifest.com/web-design/blog/6-steps-avoid-online-form-abandonment

History.com Editors. (2021, September 24). *Printing Press*. HISTORY. https://www.history.com/topics/inventions/printing-press#:%7E:text=Goldsmith%20and%20inventor%20Johannes%20Gutenberg,use%20commercially%3A%20The%20Gutenberg%20press

Kitces, M. K. (2020, September 21). *Client Acquisition Costs For Financial Advisor Marketing Strategies*. Nerd's Eye View | Kitces.Com. https://www.kitces.com/blog/client-acquisition-cost-financial-advisor-marketing-efficiency-lifetime-client-value-lead-generation-satisfaction/

Klein, C. (2022, May 17). *How McDonald's Beat Its Early Competition and Became an Icon of Fast Food*. HISTORY. https://www.history.com/news/how-mcdonalds-became-fast-food-giant#:%7E:text=McDonald%27s%20grew%20thanks%20to%20its%20%27Speedee%20Service%20System%27&text=According%20to%20Love%2C%20they%20simplified,volume%2C%E2%80%9D%20Richard%20McDonald%20said.

Meares, H. M. (2016, August 5). *The Real McDonald's: The San Bernardino Origins of a Fast Food Empire*. KCET. https://www.kcet.org/food-living/the-real-mcdonalds-the-san-bernardino-origins-of-a-fast-food-empire

Moran, K. M. (2020, April 5). *How People Read Online: New and Old Findings.* Nielsen Norman Group. https://www.nngroup.com/articles/how-people-read-online/

Newberry, C. N. (2022, April 18). *Video Thumbnail Guide: How to Inspire Clicks.* Vidyard. https://www.vidyard.com/blog/video-thumbnail/

Pershing & BNY Mellon. (2018, October 18). *Advisor Value Propositions: How Advisors Showcase Their Value to Investors—and What Investors Secretly Think.* Pershing. https://www.pershing.com/perspectives/advisor-value-propositions

Ross, L. R. (2022, April 25). *Why Welcome Emails Are Important – Statistics and Trends [Infographic].* Invesp. https://www.invespcro.com/blog/welcome-emails/

Shampanier, K. S., Mazar, N. M., & Ariely, D. A. (2007). Zero as a Special Price: The True Value of Free Products. *Marketing Science, 26*(6), 742–757. https://doi.org/10.1287/mksc.1060.0254

Shelton, J. S., & Kumar, G. P. (2010). Comparison between Auditory and Visual Simple Reaction Times. *Neuroscience and Medicine, 01*(01), 30–32. https://doi.org/10.4236/nm.2010.11004

Staff, B. (2020, March 31). *Paying Attention: The Attention Economy.* Berkeley Economic Review. https://econreview.berkeley.edu/paying-attention-the-attention-economy/

Zenger, J. (2017, January 13). *Steal These 3 "Speed" Strategies For Leadership And Business Success.* Forbes. https://www.forbes.com/sites/jackzenger/2017/01/12/steal-these-3-speed-strategies-for-leadership-and-business-success/?sh=3d25e2a1dca0

Made in the USA
Monee, IL
22 September 2022

9bb21257-5d8f-4d10-870e-4606afa1f02cR01